Paul Harrison is one of the most popular drivers in motorsport. Starting his BriSCA Formula 1 Stock Car career in 1985, he first found success as British Champion in 1991 and 1993 and then as European Champion in 1998 and 2003. However, his primary aim was always to match his father's achievement and become World Champion. In 2011, he finally achieved his ambition at the 23rd attempt, also securing a third British Championship in the same year. He lives in Wickersley, South Yorkshire with wife Lindsey and children Bradley and Melissa.

My Time

Paul Harrison

Chequered Flag
PUBLISHING

Published in the UK by Chequered Flag Publishing
PO Box 4669, Sheffield, S6 9ET
www.chequeredflagpublishing.co.uk

A CIP record for this book is available from the British
Library

ISBN 978-0-9569460-3-4

Printed in the UK by Henry Ling Limited

Picture Acknowledgements
Mike Greenwood: pp vi, 6, 20, 36, 46, 100, 134, 164,
172, 198, 208, 274, 281
Paul Harrison: pp 88, 106
Scott Reeves: pp 62, 76, 122, 146, 182, 220, 234, 244,
256, 262, 272

For my family:
Mum, Dad, Vicky, Lindsey, Bradley and Melissa.

I'm glad that you were all there to share it with me.

My Time Has Come

So I won my semi and got to start on the front row,
Then lost the toss to Hinesey, well whaddya know,
Not always the best place to start, outside row one on
the grid,
To win the gold in my 23rd World Final bid.

And just the day before, my emotions were all over the
place,
When my mate Iain sorted me a chat with a sports
psychologist ace,
So as I woke up that morning and as I lay in my bed,

I realised that Mike Finnigan had truly sorted out my
head.

'Cos gone were my jitters, and my state of mind was
restored,
I can win this I thought, with my confidence assured,
We arrived at Northampton, I was in a positive mind,
Family, friends and fans, words of encouragement were
kind.

I went out to practice, putting the car through its paces,
In preparation for this, the most important of races,
Then it was time for the parade, as we waited at the pit
gate,
I recall Hinesey's team in a proper nervous state.

Then out onto track, as we all enjoy the occasion,
The crowd all cheering, whichever driver their
persuasion,
As we form the grid, and are asked a few words for the
crowd,
I say this is my time to win it, I wanted to do myself
proud.

I get strapped in by my team, who tell me to prove what
I'm worth,
Suddenly my cab feels like the most lonely place on
earth,

The girl with the placard walks past, just one minute to
go,
Normally I'd watch her arse in my mirror, but today I
don't want to know!

'Gentlemen start your engines' the next words I hear
mention,
The hairs on my neck all stand to attention,
I turn the engine and catch it, as it roars into power,
I'm ready, I'm focused, to make this my finest hour.

Two rolling laps, side by side next to Paul,
Thinking don't go too early, no prize for first in the wall,
Then out with the green and off we all blast,
I drop back to fourth, as Frank and Tom go past.

Soon I'm second behind Frank, and I know this bloke's
no messer,
Then the yellows come out, for Rob Cowley the
hairdresser,
He's landed on his roof, quite a terrible farce,
He of *Gears and Tears* fame, with the great bruise on his
arse.

The race gets restarted, Dan Johnson looks quick,
He seems in a hurry, so I'm in for some stick,
Yellows again, Peter Rees crashes hard indivertible,

The marshals are on hand, to make Riley's car a
convertible.

We wait on the start line for what seems like an hour,
As I stare at the start line, which says believe in your
power,
On the start Dan soon passes, leaving Andy behind,
Then the yellows again, and I've got 391 on my mind.

I make a good line, as the race gets restarted,
Dan makes a move and soon Frank's been departed,
I follow Dan, leaving Frank and Andy to fight,
My car coming good as they disappear out of sight.

Suddenly the race has changed, Dan and I can advance,
I knew to act straight away, I might not get another
chance,
I line up the car and give a hard measured shot,
I charge into the lead, sitting in the number one spot.

It's just past halfway, still a long way to go,
Dan is hot on my heels, I can't afford to slow,
The lap boards come out, I'm thinking bleeding hell fire,
If there's a God, he won't let me get a flat tyre!

And then the last lap, I check the mirror for number 4,
The last thing I need is him smashing through my back
door,

As I cross the line disbelieving, surely it's not true,
This race so elusive, belongs to me, number 2.

I pull in the middle, hearing all the noise and the cheers,
I dance out of my car, getting mobbed by my peers,
My team and my family, wife, kids, Mum and Dad,
They've all seen me do it, I'm so elated, so glad.

We celebrate and party, the world seems a much better
place,
I've achieved my life-long ambition, just to win this one
race,
And it's difficult to explain, sometimes I can't describe
how I feel,
At last I have done it, yet it still feels so surreal.

And for no reason at all it sometimes pricks my
subconscious state,
A fleeting moment of no importance, will leave me
feeling great,
Other times I stare at the trophy, seeing great drivers'
names from the past,
I feel tremendous pride to be amongst them, to be
World Champion at last.

Crossing the line to achieve my dream

1

For nearly forty years I'd imagined what it would be like to become a World Champion.

In 1982, only a few miles down the road at the Crucible Theatre in Sheffield, Alex Higgins won the World Snooker Championship for the second time. I remember watching it on television. Higgins was down by the snooker table with his wife and young child, and all the cameras were on them. He was crying. The emotion just got too much and it all poured out of him.

I was watching with my dad, who didn't have time for all the histrionics. 'What the bloody hell is he crying for?'

he announced. 'He's just won the World Championship! Look at him, he's spoiling it, there's no need for that. He ought to be jumping up and down on the table!'

My dad was never shy to voice an opinion. I reckon it's the Yorkshireman in him – he's never afraid to call a spade, a spade. He could talk about Hurricane Higgins with some insight though, because he was a top sportsman himself. Having been part of stock car racing when it first started in 1954, he quickly rose to the top of the sport and won the British Championship twice, in 1967 and 1975. The Stock Car World Championship was the one title that eluded him though, so no wonder he watched Alex Higgins with such envy. He was desperate to win the World Final, but time seemed to be running out.

It all came good four months later. In September 1982, he crossed the line first and became a World Champion himself. There might have been a few tears in the crowd, but there certainly weren't any from Dad. He was ecstatic, the happiest bloke in the world, but he stayed composed throughout and didn't let himself break down. I was a very proud 13-year-old.

I already knew I wanted to become a stock car driver. I had been racing a Ministox for the past five years. I followed Dad into Formula 1 stock cars pretty much as early as I could, three years later at the end of 1985. Since then I had competed every season and I'd had my own successes. I had won both the British Championship and the European Championship more than once. But, just like Dad,

I struggled when it came to the World Championship. It always seemed to escape me. Three times I came second and twice I came third, but nobody remembers those who get on the podium.

The World Championship was the one goal in my life, the one that I had always wanted to win. I even said to my wife that I'd rather win the World Final than win the lottery. It meant that much to me.

I always thought I'd be more like Alex Higgins than Willie Harrison. I pictured myself crossing the line first in a World Final and being overcome by a wave of emotion. I thought I would be crying as I got out of the car and when I was presented the trophy.

As it turned out, I was wrong.

*

I'm usually nervous when I strap myself into the car before the start of a World Final. It wasn't that I'd never done it before, because this particular World Final was number 23. It's the pressure of the occasion that seems to get to me.

This time it was different. There was no tension, I wasn't on the edge, I had no butterflies in my stomach. I felt good. It was the World Championship, the one that I had raced for all year, and I just felt calm and focused.

I only had one mechanic, Lee, to help me with the harnesses. The rest of the team had wished me well before I went onto the track. Lee patted my shoulder and walked off, leaving me alone in the car. I waited for the signal to fire up my engine.

When it came, 34 V8 racing engines roared into life. We moved off on the rolling laps. Paul Hines, on my inside in pole position, seemed to be going a little fast. I looked in my mirror and saw Frankie Wainman Junior behind Paul, arm out of the window, signalling him to slow down. It was Paul's first time on the front row in a World Final and he was pumped up. I thought that I was doing a good speed, controlling my half of the grid from the outside of the front row.

At the start of the back straight, half a lap before the race started, I let Paul go a little bit. He quickly came back into position, but by then I had moved across slightly, positioning my car central on the track, leaving Paul no option but to slot in tight up to the inside edge. I'd been studying the starts of races on YouTube to get a few ideas, and I'd decided I wanted Paul towards the inside of the track with little room to move about.

I didn't want to go too early, get in front and get clobbered into the first corner. I couldn't afford a bent rim or bent shocker, I needed the car 100% for the whole race. Equally, I didn't want to go too late and let everybody else get a jump on me and hang me out to dry. We slowly approached a patch of tarmac which had been freshly laid to cover a pothole, a point that I'd highlighted to myself on the parade lap and thought would be a good point to go. I booted my foot down on the accelerator. The engine screamed, but I suddenly realised it was too early, I would be on the front of a train going into the first turn. I immediately lifted my foot, but just as I did so, everybody else went – the green flags were waving and the World Final was on!

So it was pedal to the metal again, down the home straight we went. I looked in my mirror and I could see that the foreigners on the third row had not set off quite as quickly as the front four: myself, Paul, Frankie and Tom Harris. I kept wide to let Paul and Frankie go and could see Tom sweeping into the first turn behind me, so I decided to let all three through and slot into the gap before the foreigners. I stayed wide, really wide, but Paul, Frankie and Tom took a wide line too.

All of a sudden the train followed on behind. Cars pushed each other into the corner and I was engulfed. One of the foreigners scraped the back of my bumper, just at the moment where I needed to be making the turn near the fence. It twitched my back end and set me up for a good exit from the corner, so I shot up the inside of Tom a second or two after he had passed me on the inside. I had survived the first turn and only lost one place.

Down the back straight we thundered. Frankie nudged Paul to make him run wide so he could take the lead on the exit of the next corner. I was close enough to go through too as we passed the starter, meaning that in the space of the first lap I had gone from second to third to fourth to third to second!

I was looking at the back of Frankie's car. He had a reasonable gap, but I wasn't concerned. I knew that after two or three laps, the time it takes for my tyres to warm up and reach their peak speed and grip, I would be able to catch him and take the lead. That would have to wait a little bit first though, because as I began to close the gap the marshals waved their yellow flags to bring the race to a halt and rescue Rob Cowley from his rolled car.

We lined up on the home straight, waiting for the track to be cleared. I was second behind Frankie. Just above his car, across the start-finish line, was a banner. It read, 'reach for the stars... believe your own power.' I stared at the banner. It seemed to be speaking directly to me. I felt good, confident in my car, faster than Frankie. I was persuading myself that I was going to win the World Final.

Once the short stoppage was over, we rolled past the banner, round the turn and onto the back straight. Frankie went really early, more or less as we went into the turn at the end of the back straight, but I was ready and I went with him. In the couple of laps I knew it would take my car to be at full speed, I looked in my mirror. I could see that Dan Johnson was coming through the field quickly, but I was also catching Frankie. We circled the track a couple of times. I was close to where I needed to be to challenge for the lead. A cloud of tyre smoke appeared where Murray Harrison spun wide towards the outside of the first turn, so I aimed for the inside and blasted my way through. That was out of character, usually I would see smoke and back out of it, but this time I went for it. Frankie must have backed off a little, because down the back straight I came alongside him. Then the yellow flags came out again and I saw smoke coming from a car in difficulty. We stopped again. I looked behind and saw that Dan Johnson was now in third place behind me.

I wasn't aware that there was a problem involving Peter Rees until Guy Parker walked on the track. I overheard him telling Frankie, 'you can't get out of your car but you can take your helmet off, it's going to be a while.' When he came to my car I asked what was amiss. Guy told me that Peter had crashed and wasn't in a good way, so I could take my helmet off. I didn't, I left it on.

I sat on the home straight again, in the same position as before, behind Frankie's car and looking at the banner. 'Reach for the stars… believe your own power.' It took on such significance in my mind. It was the basis of what I had been thinking before the race. It was as though the banner had been put there for me – it even crossed my mind that it might be a figment of my imagination!

A bit later on, Guy came over again and repeated that I could take my helmet off because they were cutting the roof off Peter's car, but the helmet remained on. I was still, focused, positive. They could take as long as they liked, they could throw whatever they wanted at me, but I wasn't going to get out of the mindset I was in. The confidence I had in myself and my car would not be diminished.

After a long delay, the race restarted. Frankie went early again and shot away. I got a good enough start to keep up with him, but I had to be careful that the differential didn't give way. The Transit rear axle I raced with could cause a few problems because the differential didn't like it if you floored the accelerator to set off or changed gear too fast. I was conscious of not putting too much stress on the back axle on each restart. It was evident straight away that Dan was in a big hurry. I got a little push from him as I was brushing the apex, just as I was turning into a corner. Dan was letting me know his presence, I was under his feet, and he gave me a reasonable tap as we went down the home straight. I had two choices. I could ride my luck and potentially be on the receiving end of a big hit, or I could move aside. This was the World Final, Dan wasn't going to be hanging around and I didn't want him putting me out of the race, so I moved out of his way and he came past. I held my line well and settled in behind him, but within another lap or two my car gained speed and I was keen to pass him back. I gave Dan a reasonable nudge, perhaps a little harder than he gave me. Just as I was positioning myself to overtake, the yellows came out again. It seemed that they waved the yellow flags every time I was trying to improve my position!

This time I lined up on the home straight in third position. Frankie was still up front. In second was Dan who was travelling fast. I looked in my mirror. Now I had Andy Smith behind in fourth, then Paul Hines, then Stuart Smith Junior. Andy was the driver who I'd said before the race was the one I had to beat. He was the defending champion and aiming to be the first driver to win the World Final four times in a row. And suddenly he was up my backside.

This was the moment of truth. The next couple of laps would be the defining laps of my race. I still felt confident, but I needed a couple of laps to get to full speed again.

I needed to stay focused. There was that banner again. 'Reach for the stars… believe your own power.'

Frankie took the third restart in a similar manner to the first two, going early, but I was now expecting it and both Dan and I kept up with him. I looked in the mirror heading down the home straight. Andy was about two car lengths back. Another quick glimpse as I made the turn showed that he braked in a similar place to me going into the corner. He wasn't diving at me on the first bend. We went down the back straight and into the next turn. Andy didn't attack again. I kept a good speed through the corner, faster than I had in the early laps after previous starts, so as I passed under the starter and glanced in the mirror I realised that I'd pulled a little distance away. If Andy didn't attack me on this corner, I thought I would be ok. As I came out of the turn safely again, suddenly I felt up for it. I was relatively safe in third place and driving well.

The next time I passed the starter, I could see that Dan was setting up his car to attack Frankie. In he went, connecting with Frankie's back bumper, a good hit. Frankie rattled the wall, but Dan's car was unsettled as well and ran wide. I could see Frankie riding the wall. I stayed close to the inside and as Dan returned to the racing line down the back straight I was only a fraction off him. I looked in my mirror to see Frankie recovering from hitting the wall and rejoining just behind me, in front of Andy. If I was Frankie, I'd have got out of the way. His car was injured, but he was still trying to beat Andy down the back straight. I could tell that something was going to happen.

I concentrated on making a good corner. I breathed in, turned the wheel and just missed the kerb. It was a clean corner with a tight inside line, meaning that if Andy flew at Frankie he wouldn't hit me as well. I made it round the corner and looked in my mirror as I was going down the home straight. Something had happened because Frankie was no longer there, but I couldn't see any impact. But that wasn't my problem. Dan Johnson was.

My good corner allowed me to carry more speed down the home straight and Dan was in striking distance. I knew it would have to be a decisive move. I hit Dan hard, a good knock, as we went into the corner. It was measured. I didn't want to follow in, but I wanted Dan to hit the fence. For a moment I wondered whether I had got it right. Dan headed wide, but I was carrying a lot of speed too. I concentrated on making the turn and keeping out of the fence, but I was also aware that Dan was hitting it. As I returned to the racing line down the back straight I realised that Dan had kept it going and was within striking distance. But he didn't take a shot at me. I got another good line through the corner and went past the starter. The World Final was now at half-distance, and I had the lead.

There was no time to think. Into the next corner. Concentrate. I turned through it and was off down the back straight again. A quick glance in the mirror. Dan had dropped back, too far to get a measured shot. Remember to breathe. I knew I had to concentrate on making good laps now. Frankie was parked up and out of the race. I couldn't see Andy. As far as I was concerned, it was a two-car race between Dan Johnson and me for the World Championship. It was time to see how good my car and I really were.

Every lap, every bend, I put everything into making the car run perfectly into corners. As I caught up to back-markers I couldn't afford to wait. There was no option of giving them a tap and hoping that they moved over. Anybody who got in my way was going to get dustbinned. Marco Falkena appeared on the racing line and I sent him into the fence, but I knew I mustn't hit anybody too hard because I didn't want the waved yellow flags to come out again. Dan might have taken a bit of a knock and was seeing a few stars, but if he had time to recover and started up my backside after a caution, I'd be a sitting duck.

I wasn't thinking about winning, I was just thinking about driving good laps. Then I saw the starter show the board saying five laps to go. Bleeding hell, I had led for a few laps now, something I'd not done before in a World Final. I could tell that I was pulling away from Dan. This could be it!

I started to count the laps down. I circled the track a few more times and looked up at the starter expecting him to be holding up the last lap board. Two laps to go. Bloody hell, I was counting too quick! Another lap down, now it was the last lap. I wasn't worried about car failure. I was wondering whether Dan was far enough away. I could tell that he was a reasonable distance from me, but this was the World Final. How brave – or how daft – did Dan feel? I had already experienced Stuart Smith Junior being a boat ride away from me on the last lap of the British Championship and still coming at me, so as I went into the last corner I was watching Dan in my mirror. Surely he couldn't get at me now? Halfway round, I realised it was impossible for him to touch me.

I could see the chequered flag in the air. I lifted my arm out of the window. I was already celebrating as I crossed the line.

The wave of emotion I expected didn't come. I was just laughing. As I climbed out of the car I had completely dry eyes. Drivers came over to me, congratulating me. My team came running on. I wanted my family on track to celebrate with me. My dad was there, happy to soak up the atmosphere, although he made clear that this was my moment, not his. My wife was tearful. I said to her, 'what are you crying for? We just won the World Championship! This is fantastic! This is what I've been doing it all for. This is the goal I've been aiming for!'

I was World Champion.

About to take the lead in the World Final

2

En route to my first meeting of the season, at King's Lynn towards the end of March, I stopped the transporter bus at a service station to fill the jerry cans. I put about £80 of petrol in them. I was well aware that the cost of fuel was spiralling higher and higher, my road haulage business can live or die on the price of diesel and the recession had already hit us hard. Yet after a break of four or five months from the last meeting, it seemed like the cost of petrol had shot up again. I usually try not to take into account how much money I spend on racing because it would put me off, but the high price of fuel set me thinking. The bus does 10 miles to the gallon. It's about a 200 mile round trip to King's Lynn, so that's roughly 20 gallons. Quick arithmetic showed that it cost £120 in diesel just to travel to and from the meeting. On top of that there is the cost of racing: petrol for the car, tyres, parts and repairs. I totted up an estimate of how much it costs to go racing at each meeting, and the answer scared me.

I had spent the last few seasons moaning about the cost of tyres, yet the price of a new tyre seemed insignificant in comparison to the huge number I had just come up with. I was already spending a load of money to turn up at meetings, so saving a few pennies and running on rubbish tyres was counterproductive. I race to enjoy it, but I still want to win rather than making up the numbers.

I might as well do it properly. I decided there and then to start spending a little bit more on tyres and to run better tyres in key races rather than getting an old one out of the back of the bus and slinging it on the car just to get out on track.

I was also aware that stock car history was resting on my shoulders. Yes, I race for enjoyment, and winning isn't essential to me. But I was now in my forties and my racing career was long enough for people to make a judgement. Did I want to be remembered as a driver whose potential was greater than his ambition? The best driver never to win the World Final? I didn't want to finish my career without winning the greatest prize in the sport.

My dad is always willing to offer advice, so I sat down with him and told him what I was thinking. I said that in the coming season I wasn't willing to make up the numbers and be happy with a good place. I was going to win races, and win them well. I was going to attack the World Final.

'About bloody time!' he answered. 'I've been thinking that for 20 years! You're capable of winning the World Final, just set out in your mind what you are going to do and go out on track and apply it. Stock car racing isn't rocket science!'

Lindsey, my wife, was equally supportive, though perhaps in a less blunt manner! We met outside of stock cars, so perhaps she wasn't aware of how much commitment the sport needed when we first got together. But she has always encouraged my stock car career and never moans about the time I spend in the garage or at the track. She told me to turn the thoughts about money into something positive: 'you can win if you keep this mindset.'

So I spent a little more on tyres and went out on track with a changed attitude, attacking races rather than sitting back and letting things happen. The two combined and transpired into better results for me. There were still some meetings where I would drift away a little bit and forget that I was there to win, but afterwards I'd kick myself and realise that I should have done better. Sometimes it struck me even when I sat in the car waiting to go off the track at the end of the race, and I would feel myself get angry – why didn't I do this or that? Couldn't I have done better?

It helped that I was driving two decent cars. My team and I made some small alterations to the shale car over the winter. At the first shale meeting – that King's Lynn one where I had the nasty shock at the fuel pump – I realised we had pushed the car from being mediocre to one of the quickest. I came second in the meeting final and won the Grand National. As the season developed, it became obvious that my shale car was at its best when the track dried out in the second half of a race. As spring turned into summer, conditions suited my car perfectly. Results came my way, my confidence grew tremendously, and I carried a positive frame of mind from one meeting to the next and from one surface to the other.

Tom Harris had my tarmac car over the winter, fitting a Transit back axle and altering the engine mounting configuration to make the engine sit more securely. It had an immediate effect as I won my first tarmac race of the year. It felt like the car had a little bit more oomph coming out of the corners.

I was flying by the time the fourth King's Lynn meeting of the season came round, in June. It was the British Championship, and I was determined to give it a good crack. I did well in my heats – fourth, first and fourth – which put me on pole position for the championship race. I knew I was in with a great chance if I got a good start.

It all went disastrously wrong at first. The track was wetter than I would have liked for the final. As the green flag fell I charged down the home straight and there was a big shot from behind on my bumper. I drifted up the track towards Tom Harris, who started alongside me on the front row. The side of my car made contact with his and the pursuing pack continued to run into my back end and spun me around. I was facing the wrong direction, brushing against the fence, with 26 cars heading my way. Through sheer luck, they picked my car up and spun me back round into the right direction. The car had stalled, but I bump-started with the momentum and through good fortune was going down the back straight.

Only then could I gather myself. The wheels were okay and the engine seemed to run fine. I had got away with it, though I had dropped more than ten places. Things were still happening all around me on the wet track as I made my way round the next corner and onto the home straight again. Then I clattered Tim Warwick who was stranded on the first corner and I was forced round the outside. At that point the yellow flags came out. I had clawed my way back up to seventh in the chaos of the first couple of laps.

The car was still driving well. After the restart, I managed to steer clear as Tom Harris and Frankie Wainman Junior took each other out, while Mark Woodhull rode the fence and John Lund took avoiding action. That took me up to third, and a second period of waved yellows helped me get up with the leaders, Stuart Smith Junior and Dan Johnson.

Now I felt like I could race properly. I passed Dan soon after the restart and concentrated on chasing Stuart, but yellow flags waved again to stop the race. I sat in the car and considered my tactics. Stuart is a hard, aggressive driver and if I got involved in a scrap it would be futile. I couldn't give him the opportunity to get to my back bumper, because my race would soon be over. But I was in second place, which meant I was in the driving seat. I could decide where I would pass him and when I would open myself up to the risk of a counter-attack. For the moment, Stuart was the one with the target on his back.

Tactics are all well and good, but they often fall apart within a few metres. Dan tapped me wide at the restart, putting me in the loose. He went round the inside, along with Mark Woodhull and John Lund. The following bend I got past John and Mark, but as I tried to go up the inside of Dan, the outside of my rear bumper got stuck on the inside of his front bumper. Dan dragged me towards the fence, but fortunately we separated with me in front and I got through the corner without anybody else getting a nudge on me. Frankie had got back into the mix by that stage and the drivers behind me began to slow as they fought their own battles. Once I made another corner where I was not under pressure, I had chance to look ahead. Stuart was the other end of the straight, miles in front, and I had no option but to chase him. He still had that target on his back, but I was too far away to make any use of it.

I thought that was it. Over halfway through the race, I was in a safe second place. First loser again, but it was the best I could expect. I concentrated on fast, tidy laps. After three or four laps, the gap was visibly closing. Perhaps Stuart was just conserving his car, so I thought little of it. After three or four more laps, I noticed again that there was less distance between us. Stuart must have been able to see me in his mirror and should have started pushing again to maintain his lead. Yet with five laps to go, I was still catching him. Stuart was not running as fast as I was, and I might have a slim chance.

With two laps to go, I was still too far away. Then Stuart hesitated as he went round the turn to head into the final lap. I was within shooting distance. Game on! I was back in charge, and my next move would either win me the race or throw it away.

I had been in this situation before. Chasing John Lund to win the European Championship in 2002, I left it to the last corner and it all went pear-shaped. Last bend attacks can work well, but if it goes wrong you've lost your only chance. I decided to attack Stuart on the first turn of the final lap. I backed off slightly to maintain a reasonable distance so I didn't push him into the corner. It needed to be a proper bumper move. I hit him hard enough to send him onto the loose shale and into the fence, and I turned into the corner. As I moved onto the back straight

I looked in my mirror. I couldn't see Stuart's car, just a cloud of shale dust. Halfway down the straight, I could see that the dust had moved. Stuart had his foot to the floor and was powering round the outside. I realised he was coming at me, regardless of how far ahead I was. If it was anybody else behind me, I would have felt safe. But Stuart is all-or-nothing. I took a regular line into the last corner, and glanced again. He was definitely coming. I tapped the accelerator as I reached the apex to move my car a little further out of his way and braced for the impact. I didn't feel any bumper, but I did feel a whoosh of air behind me. He had missed!

It was a matter of a few metres to cross the line with the chequered flag waving. I was ecstatic to win the British Championship, but I was even more pleased to win it in such style – driving the best car at the meeting, earning pole position and winning the championship race despite being demoted down the pack during the race. It still ranks as one of my more satisfying victories, if not the most satisfying, and at the midpoint of the season it confirmed that I was on the right course. My car was good, I was driving as well as anybody, and most importantly my positive mindset was bringing success.

With the British Championship over, attention turned to the World Championship. With a couple of qualifying rounds to go, I was fifth in the standings. In previous years I had finished fourth, which means a position on the outside of the front row in the same World Semi-Final as the top qualifier. This time, Dan Johnson pushed into the top four qualifiers, leaving me in fifth place. I wasn't too bothered – in fact, I thought it was a result. Instead of starting on the outside of the front row, I would be on the inside of the second row. Nowhere is safe on a stock car grid, but I'd much rather be on the inside of the second row than the outside of the front.

I was even keener to avoid the front row considering that Frankie was likely to top the qualifying standings, meaning he could choose his favoured track for his semi-final. He had said that he would choose Belle Vue because the other semi-final at Skegness clashed with a Ministox meeting in the Isle of Man that his children wanted to compete at. I could see myself flying into the rope and post fence on the first corner if I started on the front row there.

Things shifted slightly at the last qualifying round, which was also at Belle Vue. Stuart Smith Junior won the final, I was second, Andy Smith was third. My car was in mint form and although Stuart got away in the final while I had a battle with Andy, I reeled in Stuart towards the end of the race and thought I might get him on the last lap again, just like at the British Championship. I wasn't quite close enough and there was no point in a suicide dive on the last bend, so I settled for second. I wasn't daft enough to throw away a podium place, though had the roles been reversed I'm sure Stuart would have had a go and they would still be pulling us both out of the fence!

Frankie had a nightmare and could not match the pace of me, Stuart and Andy. After the meeting, when the qualifying points were totted up, it showed that I would be in the same World Semi-Final as Frankie, Andy and Stuart. I considered the options and decided that there was no way that Frankie would choose to race at Belle Vue when he had just been comprehensively outraced by the three of us. If he chose to race at Skegness instead, it would also force some of the tarmac specialists in the other semi-final like Tom Harris, Lee Fairhurst and Mick Sworder to race on the shale at Belle Vue. Lo and behold, a few days later Frankie announced that he had chosen to race at Skegness.

Lining up for that World Semi-Final was almost like a World Final. The drivers on the grid had won the World Final seventeen times between them. Nobody in the other semi-final had won the World Final at all, or even had a front row start. It was very much a case of the old timers in one race and the young guns in the other.

I knew that it would be a big race. I sent my tarmac car to Tom Harris to have a four-link suspension put on the front and got it back a couple of weeks before we went to Skegness. At first the car drove like a blancmange, but after a couple of races we worked out how to alter the setup and the car felt more stable and faster mid-corner. I hoped it would help for the World Semi-Final.

A question mark hovered over what would happen at the start because Lee Robinson did not take his place on the grid. Since Lee should have started on the inside of the third row, that left a big gap behind my car. Starting on the inside of the fourth row was John Lund. I knew that he wouldn't leave the gap for long and that he could use it as a runway to launch me into the fence. I had suffered that fate from John's bumper once before in a Skegness World Semi-Final, and knew I had to avoid it happening again.

I decided to stick close to Frankie and hope that I could get round the first corner before the inevitable fireworks. I got a good start and whipped down the home straight right on Frankie's rear bumper. I could probably have got alongside him, but Frankie would have shut the door by pushing me to the inside and onto the tyres. I glanced in my mirror and could see that John wasn't charging through the gap. Stuart Smith Junior was instead. I positioned my car expecting a big hit, with the right half of my front bumper against the left half of Frankie's rear, so that if the hit came the momentum would pass through my car and Frankie would cannon off me into the fence like a billiard ball. Frankie went tight into the corner, so I had to go even further on the inside with half my car on the kerb to maintain the bumper position.

The contact came. Frankie flew towards the fence, but I followed. He hit it hard and sideways, as did I. The impact jarred the car, tears came to my eyes, but through the moisture I could make out Frankie shooting off down the back straight, his foot flat to the floor. I had to keep up with him, so I floored it too and followed him down the straight. I made it round the corner onto the home straight without anybody making contact. I quickly checked around. The wheels were okay, and the car seemed to be handling fine. Nothing was damaged.

We circled for one or two laps before the yellow flags were waved and I could check who was behind me. Ryan Harrison had moved up to third from the sixth row. I put two and two together and decided that his great progress must have been because he started the big push into the first corner. He had the bit between his teeth and this restart would give him a good opportunity to get rid of Frankie and me to get the lead. Michael Scriven and Andy Smith were lurking behind, waiting to pounce. I was willing Frankie on. I wasn't going to hit him, I just hoped that Frankie would work that out and push on so we could both escape the battles further down the grid.

Frankie made a blistering start and I went after him. Ryan was a moment too late in pushing the accelerator and didn't get as good a start. We made it round the first lap without contact. Frankie pulled out a bit of a gap, but then I closed it again. I didn't want to get into a dogfight, and I didn't want to hit Frankie too hard in case he came back at me with the red mist descending. I nudged him enough to pass him, trying to show that my car was the quicker one. I sneaked up the inside, but in case Frankie took the chance to put me out, I braked early into the next corner. Frankie nudged me wide and went back into the lead through the inside. I caught and hit him again, a little harder this time. It saw me go into the lead, but I didn't know Frankie's mindset. I braked early again into the next corner, but this time Frankie didn't touch me – he also braked slightly early. That showed me that Frankie was saying, 'come on, get a move on, let's both get away from the chasing pack.' That allowed me to concentrate on my line and I started to eke out a gap. Frankie was staying near, but the rest of the pack were squabbling and we were both safe.

I was happy with the win – a win is a win after all – but I was equally happy that Frankie had driven sensibly to allow us both to progress to the World Final. I had achieved what I had come for.

After the Belle Vue World Semi-Final, which Paul Hines won, we had to toss a coin to decide pole position. I allowed Paul the chance to call the toss because he hadn't been in that situation before. He called right and chose pole. My heart sank. I was on the outside of the front row again, a position from which I had failed twice before.

I had to make the best of a bad job. I remembered Peter Falding telling me about when he won a World Final coin toss against John Lund and chose pole. Ever the cool operator, John calmly said that he was surprised Peter took that decision because he would have chosen the outside berth. I know that it preyed on Peter's mind going into that World Final. I tried the same tactic.

'I'm surprised that you went for pole position,' I told Paul. 'I always think that the outside is best.'

'Really?' Paul's face fell. 'Why?' He laughed about it, but I could tell that I had sown a seed of doubt in his mind.

I didn't want to start on the outside of the front row. I thought it was too dangerous, that my race could be over on the first corner. There was no doubt that Paul had the advantage, but hopefully I had made him think twice. Tom Harris was behind me on the outside of the second row. As the in-form tarmac driver, the coin toss had denied him the chance to sneak round the inside and drive off into the sunset. The only person in the top four whose head was in exactly the right place was Frankie. He must have gone into the World Final very pleased with his grid position, on the inside of the second row.

Now we all had twelve days to get ready for the biggest race of the year.

Just checking it's real!

3

The week leading up to a World Final is not my favourite time of year. It's the time when I feel most doubtful, most vulnerable, most sceptical about my chances.

We made some slight alterations to the car for the last tarmac meeting before the World Final. We tried a different torque arm on the back axle, but the car performed slightly differently and I didn't have time to get used to it. Playing around with the car setup can help pick up an extra little bit of speed, but starting the World Final from the front row isn't really the time to try anything new. So in the garage on the Tuesday evening of World Final week, we switched back to the setup that we had used on tarmac all season. Other than that, it was just a case of checking the car thoroughly, making sure that the weights were right, smartening it with a lick of paint. We pumped a load of tyres up and sized them. Then the car was loaded up. From Tuesday night, everything was ready to go.

Except myself.

A few doubts began to creep into my mind. Maybe my tarmac car wasn't good enough after all? Maybe there was something missing – something that needed altering, something else that we could do to change things – but there wasn't time.

On Thursday afternoon, two days before the World Final, I travelled down to London for a function at the invitation of Iain Holden, a long-time friend and blue-top driver. We met at Sheffield train station and on the journey down talk inevitably turned to the World Final. Iain asked me how I felt about the race.

'Here we go again,' I answered. 'It's just another World Final. I've failed in 22 now, and I'll probably fail again. I'm going to go out there and do my best, but I think that if I was going to win, I'd have done it by now.'

I didn't have a good record in World Finals. Every season my focus is on winning it, but I've had so many disappointments. I had learned through bitter experience that I would build myself up for the race and come away empty-handed. When asked, I usually tried to play my chances down. Maybe it was psychological – if I didn't make a big thing of it both in my mind and in public, the disappointment wouldn't hit me so hard afterwards.

We left it at that, got to London and enjoyed the party, but the next morning conversation turned back to the World Final in the black cab on the way to the train station. Iain prompted me again. 'Come on Rubber, it's the World Final, how do you feel about your chances?'

I answered honestly. 'I'm just not up for it. I've got a lot going on at work, we're not as busy as we have been and we're going through some tough times. It's hard making people redundant. My head isn't in the right place, I don't feel up for it, and in all honesty I don't think the car is quick enough. Not at one point in the season have I sat in the car and thought: I can win this through sheer speed. Of course, I'll grab it if there is any opportunity, but to do that you need to have a fast car.'

The beer from the previous night had given me a sore head and I was on a bit of a downward spiral, but I was telling Iain what I really felt. I've never had a doubt about my driving skill, what I doubted was my ability to get man and machine working well together on the crucial day. I didn't feel that my car was quick enough.

In truth, my head wasn't right, and I had already failed before I'd even got to the track.

Iain went north on a different train line, so I had a solitary train journey to think about his parting comments. He told me, 'get your head in gear! It's the World Final, it's what you've always wanted to win, but you've got to sort yourself out if you're going to do it!'

The first time I finished second in the World Final was in 1993. My good friend Peter Falding was the only driver in front of me, and when we were stood together on the podium he said to me, 'come on Rubber, come step up here with me, it's the biggest six inches of your life!' I told him to piss off, that I'd stand on the top step when I won it myself. Since then I'd finished second twice more and got onto the podium for third place twice too. Peter was right. Those six inches really were big.

Back in Sheffield, walking home, I got a phone call from Iain. He had been busy on his train. 'I've been speaking to a friend of mine, Mike Finnigan, a consultant sports psychologist. He has a firm that do a lot of this kind of business – preparation, positive thoughts, that kind of thing. He just helped Darren Clarke win the British Open golf title, and he was in a similar situation to you. What I want you to do is ring him tonight at nine o'clock. He's at a dinner, but he's expecting your call and will take it in his car. Whether it's worth it or not, just humour me.'

That evening I went out with my wife for a nice Italian meal and we talked it over. Lindsey has always believed in having a positive mental attitude. She told me, not for the first time, that I just had to believe in myself. She urged me to ring Mike, saying, 'I don't think he'll tell you anything different to what I have been saying, but give it a go. It can't do any harm.'

I didn't quite know what to expect. I tried to approach it with an open mind, but I was definitely a little sceptical at first. I'd heard all the stories about gurus claiming to have all the answers and I couldn't avoid thinking about all the criticism levelled at Glenn Hoddle for having a faith healer when he was the England football team manager.

Back home, at nine o'clock, I rang the number. It was obvious right from the start that Mike was a very nice, genuine chap. We chatted for about half an hour. Mike asked me different questions, I gave him honest answers. I could feel myself becoming emotional, although I don't know if that's the response that he was looking for or expected.

After I hung up the phone, I went into the other room. Lindsey asked me how I felt now. Mike had brought some truths to my mind, but I didn't know just how effective the chat was. I decided to sleep on it.

The next morning – World Final day – I woke up a different person. I had gone from being a bit of a mess, my head not in the right place, to being calm and focused. All the negatives that had existed in my mind had suddenly gone away to be replaced by positives.

Lindsey and the family gave me a good luck card. I'm not a particularly emotional person, but when my daughter gave me a card that she had made herself and I saw the effort that she put into it, it brought a tear to my eye. Usually I would have thought how disappointed she would be if I lost, but now I kept it upbeat. I pictured her smiling face when I won the World Championship title.

All the way down the M1 I chatted on the bus and enjoyed some banter with the lads. When we pulled into Northampton International Raceway, we got the car out, fixed the wing on and took in the mood. The World Final meeting is always a little special with a particular buzz in the pits.

Fairly early on, Richard Kaleta came over to interview me with the television cameras. He asked me the obvious question, the same that Iain had asked the day before: how do I feel? I answered that I was feeling positive, and rather than playing the game like I had done at previous World Finals – talking up my chances and sounding positive because I thought that's what I should be doing – this time, I honestly did feel good. I felt confident, and all I focused on was the winning the World Final.

Everything that Richard asked could have provoked a negative response, but I stayed positive. He asked, 'it's spitting with rain, will that affect your strategy?' I didn't care if it snowed. I was there to win the World Final. He said, 'you're on the front row with Paul Hines but you lost the toss for pole position, is that a bad thing?' I didn't give a toss. I was going to win and I didn't care where I started. A little crowd had gathered, and as he wrapped up the interview I got a cheer and round of applause. I felt pumped.

The car went off to scrutineering to be weighed and checked, and I did four or five practice laps to take the sheen off the new tyres. It felt good. Frankie Wainman Junior was out at the same time and I could tell that I was circling slightly quicker than he was. Nothing had changed on the car other than returning to the pre-Birmingham tarmac setup, but suddenly I felt that my car was good enough and I had 100% confidence in it.

The car went off to final scrutineering and was put in the compound for World Finalists. Now I could enjoy the early part of the meeting. I watched the foreign time trials and the Consolation World Semi-Final, and I was pleased to see Mat Newson qualify and get on the grid. I always thought that if I was going to win the World Final, I wanted to have all the top drivers at the time on the grid with me. I didn't want anybody making excuses for my win.

Waiting to go out on the track for the World Final race, I looked around me. The other drivers seemed to be carrying a few nerves. I looked across at Paul Hines and his team. They looked like a group of men waiting outside the maternity unit for their wives to give birth. I felt more confident, more pumped than ever before. We were driven out to the track for the parade lap and the crowd seemed to be in good form. Then we lined up on the grid and began to get helmeted up.

A microphone was thrust in front of me while I was getting ready. I was asked again: how do I feel? My reply was broadcast over the PA system to the crowd.

'I just feel that my time has come.'

You wait for years for a gold roof,
then two come at once!

4

I just wanted to stay there and milk it. It didn't matter about the rest of the meeting, stop the clock! This was my world, and I wanted everyone to be a part of it.

It sounded odd when my name was announced: Paul Harrison, Formula 1 Champion of the World. I jumped up the steps onto the rostrum feeling as light as a feather. Cameras flashed and I got soaked through to the skin with champagne by Dan Johnson and Andy Smith.

Even as I was up there on the top step, I felt gutted for Dan. His car was flying in the World Final, he put Frankie out of the race and at that point he probably thought he was going to win. His only mistake was to leave me running.

I was glad that Andy was there too. He was a great World Champion and a good friend. He knew how much I wanted to win – I'd told him so on many occasions. I once spent Christmas Day with him and his family, discussing stock cars as we drank port and ate cheese into the small hours. We've also chatted about the importance of the World Final into the small hours on New Year's Eve. When Andy won at Ipswich in 2008, I was second. Afterwards he said to me, 'Rubber, I wanted to win that World Final, but if I was a fan I'd have wanted you to win it.'

'Rubber' is something that many people have asked about, and sometimes I've left them guessing! It simply comes down to a period when a few drivers went through a patch of giving themselves rhyming nicknames. Peter Falding decided that 'rubber ball' rhymes with 'Paul'. Some people overheard and latched onto it, probably without knowing where it came from. That's the mystery solved, although I confess I'd rather it be because of my ability to get the best out of my tyres!

Anyway, the response from the crowd on the victory parade lap was tremendous. My wife and dad were with me on the pace car and we were drinking in the atmosphere. Iain Holden was hanging off the fence – he played a real part in the win by hooking me up with Mike Finnigan. I wanted the celebrations to last forever, but I was conscious of the fact that the meeting must go on and the cars were gridded up for the next race.

Everybody wanted to shake my hand and congratulate me as we walked through the pits. It was awesome. We got to the back of the bus and there was a massive crowd waiting. Somebody had brought a gold crown from Burger King – it sat on my head for a bit, then it sat on the trophy. People wanted to come and have their pictures taken with me and the trophy, they wanted me to sign autographs. I wanted to give myself to all those people who were enjoying the moment, I didn't want to hide away and keep it to myself. I wanted everybody to have a piece of me. All my family, all the people that mean the most to me, were sat on the car enjoying the moment.

One of my mechanics passed me a bottle of lager and another one soon followed, but I didn't want to get smashed. I wanted to remember this for a long time to come. Tradition says that the World Champion is retired from the rest of the meeting so I wanted to watch the other races. There was still a huge crowd by the bus but I dashed off to the exit of the pits where I could see the track. Keith Chambers offered his congratulations, the 1995 World Final that he won now seemed a lifetime ago. Frankie Wainman Junior was there too, obviously disappointed, but he took my hand and said, 'well done, I'm pleased for you.' He must have thought I'd had a grin tattooed to my face because I just couldn't stop smiling. In no time at all the meeting finished but there was still a crowd by the bus and a throng wanting to congratulate me.

I wanted to put the brakes on the night. It was going far too fast and before long people dispersed. I headed to the bar with the trophy. The plan was to fill it with beer! It took six pints, Carl Pickering insisted on paying, and the trophy was passed around the bar. Then it was refilled and passed around again. And again. That went on all night! The bar closed at 1am but it still seemed like the blink of an eye since I had passed the chequered flag. I wanted to be there when the birds were singing at dawn!

Continuing the celebrations, my team took the party back to the pits with the Smith, Johnson and Harris families. Queen's 'We Are The Champions' was belted out several times from the back of Conrad Wilson's CW Autos scrutineering van before I headed to sleep on the bus with a smile still firmly fixed to my face.

I'd had a few beers but I wasn't slaughtered. I needed to have a clear head the next day. My intention had been to drive back home on Sunday morning and miss the World Masters meeting. I had stuff at home that needed doing and hanging around the day after the World Final doesn't normally appeal to me, but winning the World Final put a different slant on things. People expected me to stay and race and I wanted to keep absorbing and enjoying the moment.

My decision to stay was made when Andy Smith walked across the pits at the end of the World Final meeting carrying his gold wing. He passed it to me and said, 'here you go, use this tomorrow.' I held it above my head and gave it a good shake to the delight of the crowd around the bus and decided I'd fit it to my car the next day.

The next morning I got up and slowly started mooching around. It wasn't a dream, I was still World Champion! We unloaded the car and put Andy's gold wing on it. People wanted photos of me with the car and the trophy, but before long I was called out on track for a pre-meeting parade lap with the trophy. I stood on the back of the pace car with my car following me. I kept looking around at it – my car with a gold roof on. It was beginning to sink in.

I was on grid straight away for the first heat and my car felt fantastic. For a couple of laps I rounded the track, and I thought if every lap as World Champion feels like this, I'm in for a good year.

If only.

I powered down the back straight and could see Tom Harris getting a bit out of shape in the corner. He got in a ruck and was pushed wide, so I positioned myself to go up his inside. Next thing I knew, I was being pushed from behind by Danny Wainman. Danny continued shoving me into the corner, past the point where I needed to turn, and my outside front tyre connected with Tom's inside rear. Still being pushed, I started to leave the ground, over Tom's back wheel, onto his sideskid, over his bonnet, front wheel and bumper, all the time heading towards the fence. This was not what I wanted. I hit the fence hard. I could see that the front of the car was damaged and one of the tyres was wiped out. Tom tried to reverse away from me, but other cars were running into us.

It brought me back down to earth with a thump, reminding me of the reality of stock car racing – a contact sport. A marshal signalled to me and I give him the thumbs up. I was unhurt. Pissed off, but unhurt. The yellow flags came out anyway and I was dragged onto the centre green by a tractor. Tom beat me to the safe area on the infield and asked me what happened. All I could reply was, 'Danny bleeding Wainman.' He seemed to be making sure that I was having it, maybe he saw an opportunity to take both Tom and I out. But he certainly ended my race, and probably my meeting. I had to remind myself not to be too annoyed. Whatever happened, I would be going home from Northampton as World Champion.

After the race I got dragged to the back of the bus to discover that I had more damage on the car then I had got all season: bust front axle, mounting brackets, trailing arms, shocker, front wheel, back wheel and tyre. We set about fixing it all, but the meeting was going ahead at a canter with races starting and finishing very quickly. We missed the consolation, so I decided to have a more detailed look around to see what else could be done before the Grand National. On further investigation, an oil seal had popped and the back axle was bent. The repairs to the front were bodged at speed, so I decided that it was time for an early bath. I lit the barbeque, but a half-cooked sausage didn't do much to remove the deflated feeling I had.

I took my car home in bits, but I was trying to balance that with the fact that I was World Champion. I told myself to stop being such a miserable git – I had taken a lot of damage, but I was going to fix it. Nonetheless, it was still bugging me.

I'm not a driver who goes out and gets a lot of damage and I will often back out of incidents to avoid it. It's well documented that I don't like to spend a lot of time in the garage. I like to race at weekends and have a night in the garage with my mates, then spend the other weeknights at home with my family. I like cutting the grass – we've got a reasonable-sized field at the back of the house, which I trim with my ride-on lawnmower – and spending time with the children, whether that's taking Melissa to a performing arts class or Bradley to a rugby match. It takes my mind off work and stock cars.

Every Tuesday evening is a well-drilled routine. I usually finish work and get changed so I'm in the garage as the lads start arriving about six. We work on the cars for two or three hours, checking them over from front to back, ensuring that nothing is dropping off or broken, then we load up the car that I'll be using at the weekend. That means I have the rest of the week to myself. Only this week I was going to have to put in the extra hours.

Luckily, the next meeting was at King's Lynn, a shale track, so the tarmac car wrecked at Northampton could be left in the corner of the garage for a while. I only had six days to sort out a new gold wing, a job that would take a few hours, so it was a good job I didn't have to repair the car as well.

I loved being British Champion. When I won it in 1991 and 1993, the winner didn't have a special roof colour, so when I won the British Championship in 2011, I'd been racing as a red top for 23 years. Being able to display a special black and white chequered roof as British Champion was something that I was so proud of. It looked fantastic on my car and my dad could pick me out from all the other cars on track for a change!

It might sound crazy, but I didn't want to cover up the black and white checks with gold. I thought about various options, half-and-half or something similar. I talked it over with Steve Lilley, who races Formula 2 stock cars and has a space in my yard to sell vans. He said, 'you can't be half-hearted, you've got to do it gold properly.'

When we had a beer on Saturday night after the World Final, Dan Johnson told me that he would paint my roof gold, but I felt uncomfortable with that. Dan should only have to paint a car gold when it's his own. We agreed that somebody else would do it, so I rang a friend, Nathan Slater, instead. He was on a golfing holiday in Portugal. 'You'll never guess why I'm ringing, Nathan,' I said. 'I've just won the World Final and I need my shale wing painting gold. And I need it by Wednesday, because the sign writer is coming on Thursday.'

All credit to Nathan, because he told me to take the wing along to his site and somebody would look after it. The trouble was that the chequered wing had been so well painted, stickered and lacquered that it was not just a simple a rub down and paint job, it was a mammoth task at such short notice. The painter was already spitting feathers, and I was fussy about the shade of gold that I wanted. This might only happen once and I wanted it to look right. I had waited years to be gold top and I used to have certain gold shades picked out, but it has been so long that they've stopped making them! I flicked through the swatches outside in the daylight and decided on a gold, but I worried about it so much that Lee popped over to have a look and double-check my choice. When the wing got delivered I was happy. It looked mint. It was all gold with a flash of black and white checks on the underside.

Once the numbers and stickers were put on the roof, along with two stripes of black and white checks, I couldn't stop looking at it. The number 2 had pride of place – I never for one millisecond considered racing under number 1, because 2 has too much meaning for me – but as a nice discreet touch in a corner it said 'number 2 is number 1'. I had dreamt about being able to put that on the roof for years, so I was dead chuffed with how it looked in reality. Mike Greenwood happened to ring only a matter of hours after the wing was finished and asked if he could take a few photos. We positioned the car in the middle of yard, alongside Bradley's Ministox. Although Bradley had lost the Ministox gold roof a week before I won mine, we had not got round to removing his gold paint. Mike took photos of the two cars alongside each other and later sent me a disc with all his photos of the World Final and the yard photos on it – a great memento. After Mike left, it seemed a shame to load up the car because it would be another couple of days before I saw it again.

Still the events of the weekend had not sunk in. I was watching television when somebody mentioned the 'former Formula 1 World Champion, Damon Hill'. My immediate reaction was, 'lucky git.' After a second I thought, 'hang on, you're a World Champion now!' I had spent so many years being jealous of anybody else who had achieved it, and I was desperate to emulate them. Suddenly I'd done it, but it had not seeded in my brain yet.

King's Lynn would be my first meeting with my own gold wing, but it wouldn't be the first time there that my car had a gold roof! It also had one briefly at the start of the 2006 season, the first time I was going to race my current shale car. It used to belong to a mate of mine, Chris Walker, who bought it from Frankie Wainman Junior. He raced it for a couple of years on tarmac before emigrating, and I bought the car from him then. I decided to race the car on shale, so it went back to Frankie for some alterations in the winter of 2005-06. Frankie transported it to the season opener at King's Lynn, and to make sure that all was right before handing it over, he put it on the scrutineering scales the night before. I got a message from Frankie on my phone, a picture of my car on the scales with Frankie's wing on it to create an accurate reading. Frankie was the reigning World and National Points Champion, so had a gold wing with silver stripes. And the text below the photo said, 'Rubber, if you'd pulled your finger out this year, this is what your car could look like!'

The promoters asked me to take the World Championship trophy to King's Lynn for another parade lap, this time with the winner of the Formula 2 World Final, raced the night before. We arrived a day early to watch the Formula 2s and to meet up with the Smith, Johnson and Harris clans for a beer again.

The two World Finals couldn't have been more different. Mine was a fast tarmac race in good conditions. At King's Lynn, a monsoon opened up over the stadium just as the drivers started their rolling laps. It meant that the thick shale turned to a mud bath and the cars were set up incorrectly for the conditions. Still, it turned the race into a memorable one.

We stood on the back straight and I saw many of my friends have short stints winning the race: Andrew Palmer, Allen Cooper, Gordon Moodie, and then through the rain Mark Simpson suddenly appeared in the lead. Surely not! I have known Simmo for years, he is a fantastic bloke and he's had the same sort of hard luck stories that I have in World Finals. He only qualified for the big race in the Consolation Semi-Final and it was brilliant that he was on the grid, but he didn't expect for one second that he had a chance of winning. I was cheering him on, all the way to the chequered flag, happy that a driver who tried as hard as I had managed to win his World Final the week after I won mine.

We met up in the bar afterwards. There was a disco, music, beer and all my stock car mates. Simmo tried to keep it low key, but we told him to get his trophy and fill it with ale! Before long we were on the dance floor together. I was on Peter Falding's shoulders singing along to 'We are the Champions'. Watching Simmo's win helped it to finally dawn on me what I had achieved.

After the joint parade lap the next day, it was back down to business. My first race under my own gold wing was an absolute scorcher. The car was lightning fast. Tom Harris got past me early on but I followed him through the field until I was in fourth place. In front of me, Murray Harrison, Craig Finnikin and Tom were all having a good race, but I caught them. In one fantastic move I dustbinned Craig into the other two and went down the inside into the lead to win the race.

We went out again for another heat. Stuart Smith Junior had a good race and got into the lead early. I wasn't too far behind and challenged Nigel Whalley for second, but when I hit him I jumped out of gear and it took me the full length of the straight to get it back in. I would have been on to win the race if that hadn't happened, and since Stuart got docked places for jumping the start I could have won it just by finishing second. Instead of chasing down Stuart, I was chasing Frankie Wainman Junior and Ryan Harrison who passed me as I was struggling with the gears. I passed Ryan, although he tapped me wide and got his place back again. Luckily he overcooked it going into the last bend and slid wide, allowing me to sneak through for fourth.

In the meeting final I was tracking Tom Harris and Dan Johnson, who were having a right battle with each other. They were so busy dealing with each other that I could sweep into second place, where I stayed until the finish. It was a fantastic result. I followed that with third in the Grand National behind Nigel Whalley and Frankie, overtaking Ryan for third place in similar circumstances to Heat 2 when he misjudged a corner and slid wide.

It was a blistering first meeting under my own gold wing. I finished first, second, third and fourth in four races. I had come on leaps and bounds in the National Points Shootout too. I started the meeting in fourth place in the Shootout standings, 44 points behind Tom Harris at the top. By the end of the meeting, I had leapfrogged above Mat Newson and Dan Johnson into second place and halved Tom's lead to only 22 points.

It was not beyond the realms of possibility that as well as having a gold roof with black and white checks, I might have to find room for some silver on there too. The race for the silver roof has never been essential to me. It used to require a tremendous amount of dedication, and 1995 was probably my best chance. I was part of a four-way dogfight with John Lund, Andy Smith and Frankie Wainman Junior. I was leading for the majority of the months up until mid-summer, when I went on holiday to Jamaica for Anthony Flanagan's wedding to Marie Gilbank. I was the best man, so I couldn't get out of it, and nor did I want to – I had planned it for several months. I missed five meetings, and that dropped me out of the chase for the National Points Championship, a chase that it turns out went right down to the wire. Since then, I decided that the dedication required to top the grading list at the end of the season is far too much. I wanted to have a life away from stock cars.

When they brought in the Shootout, it gave me more of a chance. In ten designated rounds at the end of the season, I'm as good as anybody. Having said that, over the two previous seasons my form in the Shootout rounds was horrendous and the competition was a waste of time for me.

This year might be different. I came home from King's Lynn feeling fantastic and looking forward to the next Shootout round at Coventry. Inbetween, I also had a rare weekend off. Although the Belle Vue meeting was the first World Championship qualifying round, it was not one of the Shootout rounds. A pre-existing commitment – a weekend in Amsterdam with Lindsey to celebrate our wedding anniversary – had to come first!

Rare photographic evidence –
I do work on my car sometimes!

5

I booked the trip to Amsterdam a few days after I won the World Final. Lindsey and I like to go away for a few days each wedding anniversary, and this year it could be a bit of a celebration too. I wanted to spoil Lindsey a little bit in thanks for the help she gives me – not only in supporting my stock car racing, but also in supporting my business and bringing up our family. We still enjoy spending time together after thirteen years of marriage, both on our own and in company. And I'm sure I wouldn't have won the World Final without her.

Weekends off from racing are a rare thing during the season, so I went back to Coventry the following weekend a little refreshed. Coventry is my favourite track and my confidence was boosted when Bradley won the first race in his Ministox. My first turn on track saw me finish second to Frankie Wainman Junior. I was chuffed with that, Frankie was in a big hurry and well out of sight, but I had a good race with everybody else and came out on top. I ended up trading blows with Murray Harrison and Stuart Smith Junior, but managed to get enough distance in front of them that I could open up a little gap as they fought each other.

Feeling good about the meeting so far, I got my car ready for the meeting final. Starting from the back alongside Tom Harris, I could see that there was a lot going off in front of me – the racing was hectic from the first bend. I muscled my way through, giving as good as I was getting, and I caught and overtook Frankie. Getting past him was a good sign because he had been travelling fast in the meeting. I momentarily lost focus and went into one corner a little too heavily, with Frankie still just behind. I recovered and thought that I would be fine, but a car pulled out from the fence and trundled onto the racing line. It clipped my outside rear wheel, a light contact. I brushed it aside and put my foot on the accelerator. But there was a problem. The bump had snapped my half shaft and there was little power to the back wheels. I got round the corner, but Frankie was on my back bumper and pushed me all the way down the back straight, not realising that I was limping. He disengaged to turn into the corner and I went wide before drifting onto the centre green, race over.

I told the lads that the half shaft had gone. Half shafts for LD axles are like hens' teeth – that's part of the reason why so many people are switching to Transit axles. I did a circuit of the pits looking for a spare. Ed Neachell had one which he lent me, but when I got to the bus the lads told me that it was even worse than I'd thought – the back axle had snapped. That's all we needed. It was previously welded at Belle Vue a couple of years earlier, a bodge job mid-meeting by Mark Gilbank, so I pulled him to one side and complained that his repair had failed on me! After a quick laugh it was down to work. We borrowed Dan Johnson's welder, repaired the axle and replaced the half shaft. The clock was ticking between the meeting final and Grand National, and the marshals were flitting around to see if the car would be ready for the last race.

It was looking good until the hub nuts refused go on. The pit gate officials were being told to hang on, but I'd already given up, so I jumped onto the bus and started to make a sandwich! Then suddenly I was being shouted at, 'get your helmet on, we're almost there!' I still doubted that the team could do it, so I was going slowly, but as I got my balaclava and helmet on there was a look of satisfaction on the mechanics' faces. They were soon wiped off when the engine wouldn't start. Eventually, after a push start, I finally made it on track, not forgetting a word of thanks to the marshals who held the pit gates for me.

I wish I hadn't bothered. Maybe my head wasn't in the right place. The racing was brutal and hectic right from the green flag again. There was plenty of traffic and cars were bouncing off each other like skittles. Two or three laps in, Mark Woodhull bounced off the fence into my path and hit my outside front wheel. It was a hard contact and momentarily put me out of control, the steering wheel whipped left onto full lock, and I went shooting onto the centre green. I brought the speed down, but the car wasn't going where I wanted it to – the steering arm was broken, as was the front wheel, trailing arm, drag link, front caliper and stub axle. The axle and tracking rod were bent like bananas; the panhard rod bracket was snapped off the chassis. Basically, everything on the outside was wrecked.

I was pissed off again because Shootout points were going begging. Tom didn't finish the meeting final or Grand National and overall I gained a point on him, but Frankie had a storming night with two race wins and fifth in the final, while Dan Johnson got third in the consolation and second in the final. Suddenly I was relegated down the order to fourth again, with 21 points between the top four. If I had got away from Frankie and got a good place in the meeting final I'd have been right up there challenging Tom for the lead.

Instead, I had two cars in bits. The tarmac car, wrecked at the World Masters, had not been repaired yet. That was going to have to stay where it was because we had a week to get the shale car ready for Sheffield.

It took two full evenings to get the shale car in some kind of order, including cutting and re-welding the rear axle after the bodge job at Coventry. That Tuesday night was the latest of the whole season, going on past ten o'clock, and I was back in the garage early on Thursday evening for more repairs. I try to not let stock cars get in the way of family life and my daughter was performing in a stage show – the timing of the curtain call was non-negotiable – but I'm afraid that I turned up for her show wearing my dirty stock car overalls, with time only to wash my hands before dashing off to the performance. It was all part of the job of getting the stock car out on track. I was desperate to do the gold wing proud.

I was asked to do another parade lap at Sheffield because it is my local track, although I don't race there very often. It's not a track I consider enjoyable to race on. The trouble is that you can be minding your own business, driving along the racing line, but if other cars get off-line they hit the rope and post fence and bounce back out onto the track. Not only does it damage their car, it can damage others who are unlucky enough to be in their path – in the past I've had my back axle taken out, my sideskid peeled off, I've even had other cars in my cab, all in situations where I haven't touched the car in front and it has just got out of control.

But the Shootout meant that I had to attend. The build up to the meeting wasn't ideal. I left work on Friday lunchtime and travelled to an Eighties Weekend at Butlins in Skegness with a bunch of lads. It was a great laugh – comedians, cheesy music and plenty of beer – and by the time I left on Sunday morning I was shattered, fuelling myself with plenty of coffee. I only had half an hour at home to get changed before we were off again to Sheffield. I was too tired, and I shouldn't really have raced.

In the pits, we noticed that the front outside stub axle didn't seem to sit pretty. We decided to change it before the meeting started, but there wasn't much time. It was sorted just in time for me to get out on track for the parade lap with the World Championship trophy.

It gave me a first look at the track. What the...! You sometimes hear the phrase that a shale track looks like a ploughed field. Well, I've never seen a ploughed field looking that bad. The track was covered in thick, deep mud. Lee drove my car around the parade lap and said to me afterwards, 'I don't envy you driving on that!' It was horrific, as bad a surface as I've ever seen. The weather conditions hadn't been ideal, but it looked like the promoters hadn't done anything to prepare it.

I was back on track for the first heat. I couldn't keep the car in a straight line on the rolling lap. In front, I could see other drivers sliding down the slope on the corners. The green flag went down, I changed into top gear, but it made no difference to the speed! Ryan Harrison and Frankie had fitted Trakgrip tyres to their rear outside wheels, but I didn't have one because I wasn't expecting conditions like that. I managed to slide in behind Frankie and followed him as he ploughed a furrow that I could follow. On the corners, every car mounted the kerb – it was the only way to get any grip. A couple of laps in, the kerb had taken its toll and my rear outside half shaft snapped. Even so, we were moving so slowly that I wasn't much slower than everybody else. Usually when the half shaft goes, that's it, race over, but this time I thought I might be able to stick it out and pick up a place. The yellow flags came out when somebody went off-line and lost it, and I could see that a racing line was starting to develop where the thick shale had cleared. At that point I realised I was wasting my time because the other cars would begin to speed up, so I pulled onto the infield.

In my next heat the conditions had improved. With a new half shaft fitted, I had a steady race and finished third behind Dan Johnson and Neil Shenton. It was a trouble-free race in which I just kept on the racing line and followed Dan.

It started to get harder again in the meeting final, when it started drizzling. I was circulating at a similar speed to the others, but after about five laps I put my rear outside wheel onto the thick, wet shale. It wasn't so far off the racing line that I went into the fence, but I completely lost control and did a 360 degree spin. I set off again, but I was out of the running and I finished tenth.

It hadn't been the best of meetings so far, so I wanted to pick up a few points in the Grand National. One Shootout contender was out of the running on the rolling lap – Mat Newson's half shaft came loose and slowly worked its way out, leaving the back wheel about two metres from the side of the car! That left a bit of a gap in front of me and I had a good run into the first corner. I shut off the power and turned for the corner, but then I felt Frankie behind me. He had latched onto my back bumper when he should have been taking his line into the corner – I don't know whether he did it on purpose or by accident – but he connected with me and I went off the racing line into the thick stuff. I put my foot on the accelerator, hoping to get some grip from my rear outside tyre to propel me out, but the fence had other ideas. As it does at Sheffield, the fence seemed to reach out, grab me and spit me back out, straight into Frankie's path, who stoved into the side of my car. I couldn't get reverse gear to pull into a safe position, so they put the yellow flags out for me and pulled me onto the infield. I watched Frankie at the restart and he did exactly the same thing to another driver in the first bend, following the car into the fence, this time putting himself out. It was stupid driving. If he had wound his neck in, we would both have had decent points in the Grand National.

Frankie had annoyed me, and as far as I was concerned I owed him a DNF. And I hadn't forgotten that Danny Wainman was owed one too for putting me out of the meeting at the World Masters. Now both brothers were going to have to get it. I should have stopped in Butlins.

I'm not a bad-tempered driver and my driving style has meant that I've mostly avoided disagreements with drivers over the years. I haven't been involved in any big feuds or rivalries. Many stock car fans can recall simmering tension between Falding and Lund, Speak and Wainman or Smith and Wainman (twice!) but each of those rivalries involved two drivers who each want to be the top dog in the sport. On occasion they have not been able to stand for the other to beat them and have purposely sought each other out on track. That leads to incidents that pour fuel on the fire of the ongoing feud.

I've never claimed at any time that I want to be the ruler of the tracks. I've certainly always wanted to be World Champion, but I've never been keen to be seen as the undisputed number one – that requires more commitment than I was ever prepared to offer. Perhaps that means that I've backed off from becoming involved if there has been an incident where somebody has upset me. If an opportunity has presented itself where I can get them back, then I've taken it, but I have never gone to a meeting totally focused on dealing with one particular driver. Maybe that means that somebody has got away with it. If so, so be it.

Rightly or wrongly, it's my choice how I race; and I race to enjoy it, that's my way.

If I have had rivals over the years, it has been geographic. Peter Falding and I both grew up together in Rotherham. He was a little older and found success earlier in his career, so he was a bit like my stock car big brother. I was always the understudy, happy to ride on his coat tails to some extent.

The opposite situation occurred when Mark Gilbank came into the sport. He was another Rotherham-based racer who started a few years after me. Whereas I was happy to play a supporting role to Peter, in the early years I felt that Mark couldn't stand to be passed by me and would seek me out for special attention. Sometimes he seemed to aim his car at me when I passed him, and if he drove every single race like he did when I was just in front of him, he'd have been a world beater!

Now Mark has matured and settled down a bit. Our families go back a long way and it's good that we can now have a good race and laugh about it afterwards. His focus is now more towards his kids racing go-karts and he is more chilled out towards his own racing. The Gilbanks are one of the best prepared and equipped teams in the pits and I, amongst others, have benefited from their presence at meetings on occasions when I needed to get my car back on the track. The generous loan of their cutting equipment and welder would get my car raceworthy after damage sustained in the next World Final – and I'm sure that won't be the last time they help out.

Anyway, Frankie certainly gave me some work to do after Sheffield. Both front and back bumpers were bent, there was a bit of damage to the back of the roll cage, the rim was damaged and a tyre had burst. The frustrating thing was that it was unnecessary damage. We patched the car back together and packed up for the following weekend at Belle Vue.

Belle Vue is a shale track with totally different dimensions to Sheffield. Whereas Sheffield is almost circular, so the car is broadside for almost the entire lap, Belle Vue has two distinct straights and two definite corners where you have to chuck the back end in. However, just like Sheffield, the rope and post fence is dangerous. Everybody is a little bit vulnerable because anybody can punt anybody else off the track and into it. Drivers need to have a little bit of respect for each other, and some of the younger generation haven't learned that yet.

Perhaps thinking of Sheffield, I was expecting a wet track and fitted a good gripper on the rear inside. This time, it was drier than expected. Considering that I had chosen the wrong tyre and got hooked on Frankie at the start, I got a reasonable eighth place in my heat. But I thought I could go faster. We juggled the tyres and in the next heat I got fifth – nothing spectacular. Still hoping to find a little extra speed, we decided to fit new tyres on both outside wheels for the meeting final. The difference was noticeable. After a tussle with Frankie, I built up a bit of a gap on him. Then I made a move on Tom Harris, knocking him into Scott Davids. That brought out the yellow flags with five laps to go and I could take stock. Andy Smith was leading, he was running really well, Tony Smith was second, I was third. Behind me were Frankie, Tom, Mat Newson and Dan Johnson. On the restart I kept clear of the danger behind, got past Tony and chased after Andy. I was slowly clawing him back but ran out of laps. Still, second place in a Shootout round was pretty good.

I removed the new tyres for the Grand National, saving them for bigger races. I got a flying start and was quickly out in front of the Shootout drivers, but because I took off the best rubber, Tom and Craig Finnikin caught up and I got involved in a race with them. As I got back past Craig, Tom cocked up a little bit. I took evasive action to avoid him and ended up spinning him out. I finished fourth, although had I left my best tyres on, I'm sure I would have been in the top two.

It made a pleasant change to finish a meeting with no damage! That was a good thing, because the following week we were back in the garage to sort out the tarmac car. The next weekend would see two tarmac meetings, both Shootout rounds, and my car was still a wreck from the World Masters.

Being interviewed at King's Lynn

6

Fixing the tarmac car that had been wrecked by Danny Wainman turned out to be an even bigger job than I had expected. The back axle was refitted, the chassis was bent back into place, a new front stub axle was put in with a new disc and caliper. We decided to swap to using a rally tyre on the front inside wheel because it would last longer than the Goodyears that we had previously used. However, that affected the car setup because the tyre altered the stagger and balance of the car. We weighed the car, fiddled with the corner weights and eventually got it back legal again, but by this point the clock had gone beyond 10:30.

Another late night, they were becoming a regular thing. At least the car was packed up and ready for the weekend, and I could enjoy the Peter Kay gig on Thursday night without having to worry about it!

The first meeting of the tarmac doubleheader was at Birmingham on Saturday evening. When the car was unloaded, we weren't happy with how the front outside stub axle was sitting. I had already ordered some parts from Frankie, so I picked them up early and we got them fitted to the car. Then it was out for the first race. We trundled down the hill from the pits to the track and I tested the brakes. They were horrendous – the pedal went straight to the floor and the car barely stopped. I could tell that the first race would be a waste of time. We tried to pump up the brakes while waiting in the queue but there was no real improvement. We had messed about with so many parts in repairing the damage from the World Masters that something must have gone amiss. I did my best to race in the heat, but halfway through realised that I was well off the pace and pulled off. I could slow down a little bit, but I couldn't pull up for the corners like I needed to.

Back at the bus, we worked tirelessly to sort it. We changed the caliper again, it appeared to be working but it made no difference to the brakes. I borrowed another caliper off Andy Smith to try again and borrowed a disc from Will Yarrow. We were clutching at straws. Nothing seemed to make a difference. An ex-racer, Paul Bullock, nosed round the car while we were scratching our heads.

He suggested that the stub axle might have been bent for a while and the brake pads had worn unevenly because the stub axle was not parallel to the disc. Now that they were working at a different angle, they were twisting the caliper when the brake pedal was pressed. Changing the brake pads would solve the problem. It was worth a go. Michael rooted under the side of the bus and found some pads, but they were the wrong compound – soft shale brakes, not hard tarmac ones. They were better than nothing, so they were thrown into the car for the consolation.

For the first four or five laps, the brakes were spot-on again. After that, the compound got too hot and I was back to square one – sluggish brakes that weren't slowing me enough for the corner. I struggled round for sixth, but I was holding people up and having to pull out of their way to stop them running into my back bumper. Michael had another look under the bus and found some new hard compound brake pads. They were flung in for the meeting final, but the problem with those was that new brake pads need a heat cycle to run through and cool before they work properly. Eight or ten practice laps or a run round the pits with the brake pedal pressed would do it, but there was no time. I got out on track for the final and did a few laps while other drivers were lining up, but it was wishful thinking. There was no chance for them to cool down again.

I was battling for places and got among the red tops but became involved in an incident with Scott Davids,

Danny Wainman and Mickey Randell where we all piled together. I got going again but lost a lap. I had fitted a better tyre on my rear inside wheel and didn't want to skin that off for the sake of being a lap down, so I ran a few laps to get some heat in the brake pads and pulled onto the infield. I watched Frankie, Dan Johnson, Tom Harris and Lee Fairhurst dicing for minor places even though they were all well ahead of where I was, so I made the right choice in pulling off.

Soon I was out again for the Grand National. It still wasn't long enough to cool the brakes so they were still poor. It meant another early finish on the centre green. I was bagged off. We loaded up the car at the end of the meeting. The plan was to head off to a pub owned by Warwick Ellis, a former driver, and have a few beers. As I was driving around the pits, I asked Andy Smith if he was going. He said he was going home, so was Tom Harris and a few other drivers.

I stopped and scratched my head. Did I want to race at Northampton the next day or not? It was another Shootout round and a World Championship qualifier, but I was cheesed off. I'd had a crap day at Birmingham. The team persuaded me to race the next day, so we got on the M6 and arrived at Northampton at midnight. We watched *Talladega Nights: The Ballad of Ricky Bobby* and had a good laugh before settling down for the night. The lads had cheered me up, although I was still feeling a bit bagged off with the car.

First in the pits the next morning, we had a thorough check round the car. We tinkered with the rear brake valves, but I decided not to practise because I was still feeling fragile and I didn't want to frustrate myself if the car wasn't performing. Instead, I drove for the first time that day in the first heat – and right from the green flag, the car was superb. The brake pads had got their heat cycle and cooled down, so the brakes were back functioning as they should. I came home in third, behind Lee Fairhurst and Mick Sworder.

We put a new tyre on the rear outside for the meeting final, hoping to get as many points as possible. The green flag fell, I roared down the straight, but as I turned into the first corner Craig Finnikin came into the side of me and the back of Lee Fairhurst and it all went pear-shaped. We came to a halt. I was stuffed up the back of Lee and in the fence, Craig was on top of me, Dan Johnson was underneath. Frankie had begun it all with a massive push on the first corner and he had taken out most of his rivals. I could see Lee's car. What a mess. His roll cage, axle, and chassis were damaged, his aerofoil was wrecked. I felt so sorry for him and worried that my car would look the same. I climbed out of my cab and I couldn't believe it – other than a kinked front axle and blown inner tube, my car was fine. If I had been allowed to change my wheel, I could have rejoined the race.

I watched the rest of the final from the centre green, annoyed that I was out but thankful my car wasn't as damaged as Lee's. Frankie was flying, picking up Shootout points for fun.

With a new front inside tyre, I tried again in the Grand National. Again, Craig Finnikin came into me in the first corner and this time took me into Mat Newson. Mat spun across the front of me so I had to go the long way round the outside. It held Tom Harris back too and we were already a full straight behind the rest of the Shootout drivers. I trailed Tom as we caught and started passing the others. With a couple of laps to go, I got right behind Tom and felt a bit quicker than him. I knocked both him and Craig Finnikin wide, then got past Robert Broome on the last lap to finish fifth.

The Grand National showed that my car was back on form. It often takes a meeting to get the car right after a big shunt. The damage at the World Masters cost me the meeting at Birmingham, which I could have well done without. The Northampton meeting was better, but I had some bad luck, especially in the final.

The tarmac doubleheader had seen me drop back. I started the weekend 40 points behind Frankie in the lead. I had kept fifth place but was now 67 points behind.

The next meeting, at King's Lynn, gave me an opportunity to visit our holiday home in Norfolk. We travelled down on Wednesday afternoon and spent a relaxing couple of days by the sea. On Saturday, I got to the track early. The promoter asked me to arrive a little early to autograph some posters he had printed. Sat right by the entrance, I signed my name almost constantly for an hour and a half. I could have stayed longer but the racing started and I had to go out for my heat. It was good to meet the fans, many of whom told me that they had watched me win the World Final a couple of months earlier.

Meeting the fans and having some friends attending from Norfolk meant that I was up for doing well at the meeting. The track was a little wetter than I would have liked and Mat Newson blocked my way in the early stages, but I struggled into sixth by the end. I suggested a couple of alterations to the car which would help it grip the wet shale. Again, the Shootout drivers were keen to get away, but that meant Craig Finnikin, Dan Johnson and I only ended up holding each other up. Once I forced my way out, I finished fourth. It was an improvement, but over the last few laps the car was making an ugly grinding noise from the driveline. I figured it must be coming from the gearbox, differential or perhaps the rear outside wheel bearing that we occasionally had trouble with.

Travelling back through the pits, the noise got even worse. The meeting included a show by a Bigfoot monster truck, so we had a bit of time to work out the problem and could go at it logically. We dropped the prop off and ran the engine with the car in gear. The noise wasn't coming from the gearbox. Next we had a look at the rear outside wheel bearing. That was intact. It must be a problem with the differential or the pinion. Earlier in the season, we had a problem with a pinion bearing which had collapsed, chucking out smoke. We had a look at the pinion and found that the bearing was the cause of the noise. Problem identified.

But what was the solution? We thought we had a spare bearing, but couldn't find one in the bus. Just like the previous weekend, the part we needed seemed to have gone AWOL. I did a circuit round the pits looking for a spare, but nobody had one because it was an LD back axle. It looked like I might miss the final of the penultimate Shootout round. Frankie had the car of a Dutch driver in the back of his truck which had an LD back axle, and said that we were welcome to take the bearing out of that. It would add extra time having to extract it from a different car first, but that was our only option. Just as we were about to start, Mick Harris appeared with a pinion bearing. There was no time to spare – we bunged it into the car and put it back together as they were holding the pit gate. Eventually I got out on track. Had we been forced to rob the pinion bearing from the Dutch car, I never would have made it in time for the final. Mick was our saviour!

The race began with all the Shootout drivers looking to get a good haul of points to take into the last round. After five laps, the yellow flags were waved. I was behind Tom Harris, whose rear bumper was slightly bent, so the marshals asked me to run into it a couple of times while Tom had his foot on the brake to try and straighten it. I did as I was asked, only for the marshals to tell Tom that he would have to pull off because he had received outside help! It was a harsh decision. I could see no real problem with his bumper, it was still securely attached. He should have been allowed to carry on racing without any interference from the marshals.

Only a couple of laps later, the yellows were waved again. This time I was behind Frankie. I could see that his panhard rod was broken and it was only a matter of time before he retired or lost a tyre, so I quickly got round him on the restart. Yet another Shootout driver was in front, this time Mat Newson. I had benefited from good fortune as Tom and Frankie dropped out, but Mat was going to make me work hard. I fought with him all the way through the second half of the race but couldn't find a way through. Eventually, the chequered flag signalled the end. I could see that Craig Finnikin, Dan Johnson and Mat passed the line in front of me. As it turns out, Mat was a lap down, so I had a place on the podium. Even though any points seemed like a bonus after I nearly didn't make the race, it still wasn't enough to keep me in the running for the Shootout.

I tried to salvage something from the meeting in the Grand National, but that plan came unstuck quickly. I travelled down the back straight after a few laps with yellow-top Nigel Harrhy in front of me. I should have banged him wide, but instead I got too close and pushed him through the corner. Nigel started to lose the back end and his car slowly slipped sideways, blocking my route. It was the second time that Nigel had forced me to stop and reverse away from him at King's Lynn this season. As I planted my foot back on the accelerator, watching the other Shootout drivers go down the straight ahead of me, I cursed Nigel and vowed that he would not get the benefit of the doubt a third time. He would be heading into the fence.

I was mad, but I hadn't learned my lesson. Within a couple of laps I caught another yellow top, this time Barry Heath. I should have slotted him, but instead I gave him a small knock wide. Barry skewed back across the racing line, giving me nowhere to go. My front outside wheel contacted just behind his inside rear. Barry should have turned to the right and driven away, but instead he panicked and turned towards the infield. If I had kept my foot on the accelerator I could have crawled over his front bumper and potentially rolled over. Instead I had to stop and reverse off for the second time in the race. By this time I was totally and utterly cheesed off. I got going again, cursing because I had made a mess of the race.

I was disappointed in my performance. The car had run well during the meeting, but I didn't do it justice. I had left myself a mountain to climb. With one round to go in the Shootout, I had only closed the gap by two points to 65. The final round at Belle Vue was worth double points, but the three real contenders for the title were Frankie Wainman Junior, Dan Johnson and Craig Finnikin. They were separated by only eight points.

Celebrating success at the BSCDA dinner –
Mum and I, Lindsey and Dad.

7

You heard it here first. The silver roof was unfairly won after a murky conspiracy emanated from Leek!

I travelled down to the West Midlands the day before my penultimate meeting of the season to celebrate Ed Neachell's marriage to Zara. There were plenty of familiar stock car faces and the beer was flowing, it was just like the bar at a Coventry stock car meeting. The buffet came and went but nobody paid much attention to it. Everybody was happy with the liquid refreshment.

Pumped up by the beer, Craig Finnikin was first onto the dance floor. He led an enthusiastic group of disciples –

Ed, Stuart Smith Junior, Dan Johnson and myself among them – in a Russian Cossack dance, squatting down on our haunches and kicking before leaping up like a coiled spring. Craig has the benefit of youth and is built like a racing snake, so the sweat was dripping off us as we tried to keep up with him. At least I didn't suffer the fate of Ed and Dan, who finished the evening with ripped trousers!

The next morning I slipped my legs out of bed and nearly fell over. They were like jelly! I hobbled down to breakfast and to the car for the drive back home to pick up the bus, then back down to the Midlands for a meeting at Coventry.

Dan Johnson's bus pulled up alongside us in the pits and he limped out. 'What have you done to Dan?' his team asked. 'He can barely walk!' Ed was the same, and Craig claimed to be suffering too – although he was moving suspiciously well.

Struggling to walk and with a cloudy head, I didn't have a good meeting at Coventry. The track was just how I like it with nice, dry shale, and I initially thought I could have a cracking evening. But from the first race, the Grand National Championship, the car handled poorly. It was pushing into corners and the back end was not flicking out as it should. I started on the sixth row and progressed to fifth, but that was only the result of other cars crashing out.

We tried adjusting the tyres and stagger in the hope of being closer to the running in the second race, this time the World of Shale championship. Again, it was rubbish. The changes hadn't made a difference. I got leathered into the first corner and every corner after that for the first three laps until Mark Gilbank climbed onto my sideskid and stuck on. I clambered back to eighth place, but things weren't going my way.

I didn't even finish my heat, pulling off after a lap and a half with a broken half shaft. That was the third half shaft to go on the shale car in five meetings. It was time to sort out what the problem was.

The first time the half shaft went was the previous meeting at Coventry, when I also snapped the axle and quickly welded it together to get the car out for the Grand National. After that meeting, we cut and re-welded the axle back at the garage in a more permanent repair. We must have pulled the outside of the axle too far forward, putting extra pressure on the half shafts and changing the handling so the car was pushing into the corners. We needed to adjust the lead on the axle, but the welded repair meant that it was already as far back as it would go on the outside. The only solution was to pull the inside forward to compensate, but we didn't have time to do anything before the next race. Despite handling like a dog, third place in the consolation got me into the meeting final.

We managed to fit a shorter inside trailing arm before the final and it counterbalanced the outside being too far forward. It was much better after that, the car handled corners with ease and I was soon picking off cars in the final that were previously leaving me standing. I got round a few laps, but there were plenty of racing incidents to be aware of. When I backed off in one corner to avoid a collision, I was punted from behind, twisting the car past the cornering angle. I straightened up and cut across the corner of the infield, back onto the straight, booting the accelerator to get back up to racing speed. As the revs hit the top end, the engine started to splutter. I circulated for a lap hoping that it might clear itself. Nothing changed, so I pulled onto the infield. At lower revs, the engine seemed to recover, so I pulled back onto the track. The engine started to struggle as soon as I tried to pick up speed again. Back onto the infield.

At the end of the race, I fired up the car. It was still making awful noises, so I got a tractor to push me to the pits. I lifted the bonnet and tried to turn the engine over, but the fan was not spinning. That wasn't a good sign. Further investigation showed that the front of the engine had dropped when the impact from behind jolted the car, and the fan was stuck on the cowling. We packed the car into the bus. This would take a bit of work to sort out.

Remember Craig Finnikin, the dancing Cossack? He took an easy win in the World of Shale and his heat. He recovered from his supposedly-stiff legs suspiciously quickly!

The next week, my legs were even worse and going up stairs was agony. I hobbled around the garage to take another look at the shale car. With only one meeting to go, the last Shootout round at Belle Vue, I wanted the car in top form. I could see that the engine had dropped because the lugs that the mounting bolts attached to had both snapped. The only real solution was to take the engine out, not a two-minute job, especially considering it was just for one meeting. Added to that was the mysterious misfire, which was probably because the engine was leaning and the carburettor was being overloaded with petrol, but we couldn't be certain.

It was time to get the old warhorse out of storage. A 540 big-block engined shale car was sat in a container and last saw action at the end of 2010. It had been replaced as my first-choice car in 2006 when I bought the small-block car from Chris Walker. Big-block engines are useful on some shale tracks because you can shut off at the end of a straight and throw it in a corner, getting a pendulum effect, but I was a definite convert to small-block engines. With small-block power, the engine picks up quicker, the car is nippier and I can drive on the edge a little more.

I took the car to Belle Vue with my legs finally recovering. It was just a pity that the car was also a little stiff after a year off. The brakes were very poor in the first heat. I pulled back into the pits and explained the problem. The lads were not very sympathetic, telling me that they had said the brakes should have been checked in the garage. I even considered loading up there and then, it was that bad. It was a miracle that I got fifth in the heat – everybody else must have been driving really badly for me to have managed that!

We altered a few things and bled the brakes to try and get the back brakes functioning. They were a little better in the second heat. Now I needed to get used to the driving style needed with the big-block engine. Unfortunately Belle Vue, with its distinct straights and corners, is the shale track that the big-block is least suited to. At least I got a few laps in since the Shootout drivers seemed to be sitting back and waiting for the final to play their trump cards. I was getting more used to the car as the meeting was progressing.

A solitary fifth from two heats meant that I was out of the running for the silver roof. I decided to stay out of the battles in the meeting final and to race for points, trying to catch Tom Harris in fourth place in the Shootout standings. I sat behind Mal Brown and Joe Booth for quite a while because I didn't want to get into the middle of them while they were battling and get levelled into the fence. An opportunity arose to pass them both and get away cleanly, so I sneaked through into fourth by the chequered flag.

Going into the Grand National, there were still three drivers in with the chance of the silver roof. Frankie was in the lead, Craig Finnikin had jumped into second place with a win in the meeting final, Dan Johnson was third. It was all set up for a great finale. I would rather have watched from the sidelines!

I wanted to get going and get away from the action as soon as possible. I didn't see Dan rifle Frankie into the fence, but it was fair payback for the incident at Northampton where Frankie put Dan into a pile-up. Yet Dan still needed to have a blinder and for Craig to do very little.

I had a good race with Tom Harris. I was in front of him for a while, but Tom passed by when a couple of back markers slowed me. I could have sent Tom into the fence at any time, but I was happy to follow him. Tom had worked on my tarmac car both before and during the season, and I didn't think that it was the sporting thing to get rid of him. I didn't realise that the difference in the Shootout standings was such that if I passed Tom I would have finished above him – he ended up one point ahead – so I should have just gone for it. Even if you mug them on track, you can always buy them a pint in the bar afterwards!

The big winner was Craig Finnikin, who did enough to take first place in the standings for the first time at the end of the final race in the Shootout series. He was far behind halfway through the series, but was great in the final rounds. And I think that crippling his opposition on the dance floor gave him the momentum he needed for the final push for the title!

I was ready for the end of the season. It was time to put my feet up. Unlike Craig, I had struggled for the last couple of months. My motivation dropped and that meant my meeting average dropped too. Part of it was due to the Shootout. I would have liked to win the Shootout so I could become one of the drivers who had won the three main titles in one year, but it was not a priority. The other drivers were more committed, both in terms of car preparation and on-track racing.

There are positive aspects to the Shootout. It makes winning the silver roof more achievable for a wider group of top drivers and maintains interest in the final few meetings, but I would like to see the financial rewards amended to reflect the costs of competing in it. Everybody goes mad during the Shootout. It's entertaining for the crowd, but it gives the drivers a lot of grief. A lot of damage is sustained, with some races seeming more like bangers than stock cars. Take Lee Fairhurst's tarmac car as an example. If the Northampton meeting at which his car was wrecked was not a Shootout round, I'm certain that the incident would not have happened. Damage happens and is part of stock car racing, but the Shootout prize fund is not sufficient compensation.

Even if a driver survives unscathed, it can still cost money. Some will use two new rear tyres and one new front tyre every meeting. A driver might do well and win £1000 for coming third in the Shootout, but he will have spent a damn sight more than that on tyres alone.

Sponsors have thrown money at the series, but the promoters don't. They are the ones who benefit from the bigger crowds and spicier racing that the Shootout creates in the colder autumn months. It would be nice if a little more of that bonus came our way.

Anyway, I was happy with the season overall. Being World and British Champion was beyond my wildest dreams. I could watch the soaps on television and forget about stock car racing for a few weeks!

*

Not that I would be spending the next five months creating a groove on the sofa. I still had plenty to do, much of which came from winning the World Final.

The end of season dinner held by the BSCDA, conveniently just down the road in Rotherham, was a proud moment. All the drivers who had won competitions over the past year were honoured, and I went up for the British and World Championship presentations wearing a rather snappy gold tie, complete with black and white checks. To top it all off, I was voted Driver of the Year by the membership – an achievement which I was very proud of.

The annual dinner held by the Bradford Odsal Stock Car Supporters Club was another occasion in which I could revel in my status as World Champion. I was asked to give a short speech, so I took the opportunity to indulge my creativity and write a poem. It's something I've done for years – write silly odes and ditties for certain occasions and then perform them in front of a crowd, usually after a few drinks!

Another time to write a poem came about at Andy Smith's retirement party. Andy announced his decision soon after I won the World Final, although I'd been aware of his intentions for some time. He had lost interest. A lot of it was to do with his father's premature death. Andy had always loved being part of a family that raced, but his dad was the driving force behind it. Stuart Senior was as avid a fan as my dad, he loved stock car racing. Without him, I think Andy realised that there are other important things in his life, especially his wife and daughters. He had accomplished far more than he ever expected to in the sport and there was nothing else left to win.

I'd miss Andy at the tracks. We'd messed around in the pits when we were growing up, slowly learning about the sport that we'd both enjoyed being a big part of in later years. Being asked to say a few words meant a lot.

However, there was one event that I was asked to attend that was a far heavier responsibility than Andy's retirement party and the BSCDA and BOSS dinners put together. Along with the Mayor of Rotherham and a couple of former contestants, I was asked to be a judge to help choose the next Miss South Yorkshire! It was a hard choice. Did I stay at home on a Wednesday evening and watch a bit of television, or did I want to sit in front of a parade of beautiful girls? Purely based on the fact that it would raise a bit of money for charity, I accepted the invitation.

On the evening that I helped out, the contestants were asked to showcase a talent. We watched a video of each girl doing their thing – singing, dancing or the like – and asked them a few questions afterwards. I wasn't a Simon Cowell or Craig Revel Horwood. I was a fair judge who was able to give a compassionate mark to each girl purely based on their talents and not in any way based on their looks. That's what I told Lindsey, anyway!

Harrison first, Smith third – the World Final podium

An Ode to

Andrew Smith

Andrew Smith,
a Rochdale lad;
Born to Hilary, his Mum,
and Stuart, his Dad;
When Andrew arrived,
their family became three;
In nappies he was off to race,
perched on the Maestro's knee.

Soon toddling round the pits,
his fun on a Saturday night;
Jumping in the puddles,
and falling in the shite;
Pulling shale off cars to make mud pies,
this art he soon had mastered;
Then cheering out loud when his dad stuffed mine,
the horrible little bastard;
Staying up late playing outside the bar,
our dads would be on the beers;
The fans gone from the terraces,
so ours the only boos and cheers;
Being good all week and doing as you're told,
can sometimes be frustrating;
But we're not daft, we know the score,
'cos at weekends we go racing.

To race a Mini with his mates,
was Andrew's next request;
The Hodgsons and young Frank to beat,
to prove that he was best;
The Minis were a good learning curve,
and racing is what he desired;
But alas it wasn't as easy as that,
'cos his dad was by now retired;
So he started helping Peter,
to get his stock car fix;

And then he raced a Hotstox,
and showed off all his tricks.

When not racing we'd be out on the beer,
doing our best to pull;
Holidays abroad, nights around the country,
those times were never dull;
Then one young lady caught his eye,
to begin with it was a non-starter;
He soon changed that with his charm and wit,
and cracked it with Lisa Harter;
Around this time, he borrowed Higgi's car,
and soon made the transition;
Into F1 stox, with lots of his mates,
a popular decision;
He was soon affirmed,
as being one of the drivers to beat;
Winning gold in '94 and silver in '95,
both of which he'd go on to repeat.

And so throughout a tremendous career,
he's won races and titles galore;
Five gold, four silver, three British to show,
over 100 finals and more;
His battles with Junior Wainman,
became legendary over the years;
With Sam and Lisa being best of friends,
as we saw on *Gears and Tears*;

His brother had arrived on the scene,
to be top dog they would wrestle;
Stuart battled Andy on the track,
and in the garage wound up Cecil;
And as Andy retires from racing,
it's a sad loss to the sport;
But while Steve Rees is a promoter,
it's not the end I would have thought.

He's a family man and wants a change,
to pursue a different life;
With kids Jess and Rebecca,
and Lisa his loving wife;
His race boots not required,
it'll be slippers for Christmas instead;
Plus a flat cap as opposed to a helmet,
to cover his balding head;
A superb bloke, with bags of talent,
who around the tracks will be missed;
But I'm sure for years on Stoxnet,
his arse will still get kissed;
It's a big wide world and for now at least,
his last stock car has been bent;
And whatever destiny has in store for him,
I'm sure he's feeling CONFIDENT!

My Kiwi car sporting number 1 and a gold fin

8

One of the biggest events of the winter was still to come. I was given a gold envelope after I won the British Championship. Inside was a formal invitation to compete at the Superstock World 240 Championship, the biggest event in New Zealand stock car racing, held during the UK off-season. It was an interesting proposal, but too early for me to give it serious thought. After winning the World Final, I was given an identical gold envelope with the same invitation inside. Now I had the chance to travel to the other side of the world as World Champion, and it was much more tempting.

Seventeen years had passed since I last competed in New Zealand. Then I was a young bachelor who enjoyed the bars and nightlife as much as the racing. Now I was married, and I wanted to take Lindsey over there to experience a different country and their way of life. We put the arrangements in place. The kids would stay with their grandparents while Lindsey and I flew over for a couple of weeks so I could compete in the World 240 Championship and the 248 Global Challenge the following weekend.

In the weeks before we travelled, I was in regular contact with Sonia Hickey, the promoter at Rotorua who was organising the World 240 Championship. She arranged for me to race a car owned by Lance Ashton and built by Scott Hewson, who has a fantastic record as a car builder. That fell through because Lance's new car was not going to be ready in time for the championships, so he would need to race the one that was booked for me. Sonia made a few calls and found an alternative car owned by Graeme Barr. I knew Graeme from his time in the UK in the late eighties and early nineties and trusted his reputation as a clinical car builder, so that was good enough for me.

The mammoth journey began at Manchester Airport. Lindsey and I flew from there to Heathrow, where we bumped into Frankie Wainman Junior and Guy Parker, the manager of the British Lions stock car team that would compete in New Zealand later in the month. We had a coffee and brief chat before we separated again –

they were flying with Virgin, while Lindsey and I were with British Airways. We flew to Bangkok, then after a couple of hours in the airport were back on board and bound for Sydney. There we met up with Frankie and Guy, who both looked as fresh as daisies. Guy works for Virgin and pulled a few strings to get him and Frankie in first class. They were stretched out on their beds, enjoying the champagne, while Lindsey and I tried without much success to doze in cattle class!

After the final hop from Sydney to Auckland, we met again at Auckland Airport. Guy flew on to Palmerston North while Frankie, Lindsey and I picked up a car. We drove over to Rotorua, about a three hour journey. Frankie and I sat in the front having a good chinwag. It was good to catch up with him in a social setting because we usually have a more professional builder-customer relationship, and we talked about a lot of things that happened over the season. In Rotorua we went straight to Stan Hickey's yard so Frankie could have a glance over his car. Lindsey and I left him to it and headed to our hotel. The other British driver racing in the championships, Mick Harris, landed earlier in the day with his wife and kids. They were staying in the same hotel but had already given up and were tucked up in bed. I was really struggling too because the long journey and jet lag was beginning to get to me. It was a good job that Lindsey kept me talking during dinner, otherwise my forehead would have been on the plate!

After sleeping like the dead, the next morning I had to be back at Stan's yard for radio and newspaper interviews as part of the build up to the World 240 Championship. The reporters brought up the fact that I had been to New Zealand twice before, but it was a long time ago, 17 and 18 years previously. My first impression was that not much had changed but everybody looked older! I was pretty honest. I was there for the experience and to give a good account of myself, I didn't think I stood much chance of winning.

That evening it was the qualifying session. Sixty or so Kiwis raced in three races and the results were collated to find the qualifying drivers. Frankie, Mick and I were already seeded through to the second evening with Peter Rees and Dale Ewers, but we needed a chance to get acquainted with our cars. I saw mine for the first time in the pits. Any worries I might have had went as soon as I sat in it. Seventeen years before, I borrowed a car from Kevin Free. He was shorter than I was and I found it very difficult to drive because I was cramped up. This time, the car seemed just right. People had assured me that the car would be great because Graeme is a perfectionist, and how right they were. His team were also very friendly and welcoming, and willing to do whatever they could to help.

Frankie, Mick and I went out for a few test laps between two of the qualifying races. I needed to get used to the car, especially to left-foot braking which I would be doing for the first time in a stock car. The track was quite rutted and I struggled to control the steering wheel when it hit the bumps because it was slightly too far from me. Back in the pits we fitted a two-inch spacer to bring the steering wheel closer. It felt better, but I didn't have a chance to test it on track because the heavens opened and the meeting was rained off. The final qualifying races were postponed to the start of the following evening.

We had some free time before the championship meeting, so Lindsey and I travelled a short distance to Whakarewarewa, a geothermal park with hot water geysers and a Maori village. I tried to relax and forget what was coming in a few hours. New Zealand racing is hard with a lot of brutal hits, but there was no point in dwelling on it. I had come out to enjoy myself, not get wound up. As evening approached, we returned to the track. There were a few more familiar faces in the pits and a bigger crowd in the stands. With the qualifiers finally complete, there was a briefing where each driver picked up a sash with randomly-drawn grid positions on. It works out that each driver has roughly the same amount of cars to pass over the three races of the evening. Usually it means starting one race from the front of the grid, one in the middle and one at the back, although you might start all three races from around the middle. I drew grid positions 2, 15 and 24. I would be on the outside front row for the first race, just like the World Final. That did nothing to calm my increasingly tight nerves.

I had doubted that the outside front row was a good spot for the World Final, although it turned out well in the end. I was even less sure that it was a good grid slot here. At Rotorua, the start-finish line is not far from the exit of the final turn, a third of the way along the home straight. It has two long straights and two tight corners, a little like Belle Vue, but one corner is tighter than the other, so the track is shaped like an egg. The tight corner is the one at the end of the home straight.

I carefully watched the starts of the qualifying races to try to pick up a few tips. They were a real spectacle! All the races were clutch starts. After the grid lined up, the starter held up a yellow flag and everybody engaged gear. Then the starter swapped the yellow flag with the green flag and held that high for a few seconds. When he dropped the green flag, everybody shot off at once. Unlike a rolling start that allows cars to spread out a little more, the New Zealanders all arrived at the first corner at the same time. Carnage! It's as though somebody picks up the grid and throws them at the first corner.

Rolling onto the grid at the head of the field, knowing that I had never done a clutch start in this car and I would be right at the front as we went into the first corner, I felt like I was in the First World War trenches waiting for the whistle to go over the top. I knew what was in store but there wasn't a lot I could do about it. The cars on the inside line were more or less in the middle of the track, the cars on the outside were sandwiched between them and the wall with only a few inches on either side. To my inside on pole was Scott Joblin, a driver who won this title a couple of years before and who wouldn't make it easy for me. Graeme's team had briefed me on the start procedure. They told me to select gear when the yellow flag was out, start picking the revs up when the starter held up the green flag, and as soon as the green fell I should yank the clutch out, bang the throttle fully down and go like stink. There are only two gears and some drivers choose to leave it in bottom gear until after the first corner so they can concentrate on what was going on around them. I decided I was going to change up before the corner, three-quarters of the way down the straight.

The starter held up the yellow flag and suddenly there was a long, ear-splitting scream from behind me. It sounded like most of the other drivers had engaged gear, put their foot on the clutch and were already revving the engine flat out. The noise was phenomenal! I wasn't going to risk wrecking the engine, so I waited until the starter held the green up before starting to rev. When he dropped the flag, I reacted as quickly as possible. I got a superb start, managing to change gear where I wanted to and getting a couple of yards lead over Scott. Putting the rest of the field out of my mind, I concentrated on my own line through the corner and came out of it in first position. I was aware of the melee behind me, but had to get my head down and concentrate. I led for a good few laps until Graeme Barr managed to pass me. Simon Joblin also gave me some attention, catching me coming out of the first corner onto the back straight and feeding me into the wall. The advice I had been given if I started riding the wall was to calmly lift the throttle and drive off rather than trying any heroics and steaming along it. I dropped off and settled behind Simon, only for a stray rock to be lifted by one of his tyres and shoot through the mesh windscreen. It clattered into the jaw of my helmet and really made me jump.

I was still in third when the starter showed the white flag, signalling one lap to go. As I passed him, the throttle jammed shut and the pedal would not press down. I shifted to a tight inside line round the first corner and tried shoving it down hard. It still wouldn't move. I realised that the rock that hit my helmet must have got stuck underneath, so I tried to sweep it clear with my left foot. I found it as I was entering the final turn, so I'd done half a lap drifting round with little power. I blasted to the line but half a dozen cars had already passed and dropped me to eighth place. I was gutted. It should have been a really good position; instead I was in the pack.

Next time on track I started from the middle of the grid. These are the cars that have nowhere to go in the carnage of the first corner. I decided not to do anything stupid, I would try and pick my way through it. I had a reasonable race, there wasn't too much grief or hassle from anybody and I kept to myself. I finished seventh, a good result considering the grid position, with no damage to the car.

That consistent race paid off, because going into the third and final race I was tied for sixth place with Malcolm Ngatai and only five points off the lead. At this stage, drivers from the same home tracks get together and work out the best strategy for one of their drivers to win. Frankie and Mick had picked up a little damage so I was the highest-scoring overseas driver. In fact, I felt like going and getting the rock that had been stuck under my throttle and giving it a kiss – if it hadn't been for that I would probably be in the lead and that would mean I would have a huge target on my back for all the other drivers to aim at. Tom Harris was in that position in 2010 and got blitzed in the final race.

I had plenty going round in my head. I needed to know who was in front of me in the standings. I had been given a list of cars to watch out for, drivers who would likely be gunning for me. Added to that, just before I went out, Lindsey came to find me. She had been rung by Bradley, who was watching a live stream of the championships on the internet. It was 6am and he had his laptop set up in McDonalds with a group of lads who were going to the Autosport show at the NEC. He had just seen Malcolm Ngatai interviewed and when they asked him what he was expecting from the last race, he said, 'I'm going out there to get a pom!' I didn't need to know all this. I wanted to go out and do my own thing rather than worrying about all the other cars and drivers.

There was a big pile-up on the first corner which I manoeuvred around to pick up a few places. Suddenly I was in with a real chance. At one point a car drove me up the wall. I went right up it and landed hard on all four wheels. I could tell that something wasn't quite right; it turned out the offside front shock absorber was broken. I just knew that I was damaged but still running. One or two more tried to attack me, but I rode their hits and kept running. Then I found myself behind Malcolm Ngatai. That was all I needed. If I got past, he had made clear he would plaster me into the wall. If I stopped behind, I was an easy target for the others. I didn't want to dustbin him because I had another race meeting the following weekend and I didn't want to be making enemies and risking big damage to Graeme's car. As all that was going through my mind, Malcolm pulled off onto the infield. I was able to race on to the end unhindered.

The crew were chuffed. I had completed all three races and taken little damage except for the damaged shock absorber. They could concentrate on getting Graeme's own car fixed for the following weekend. It needed some attention because he started the final race in joint-second place but got destroyed in one of the early laps. After about half an hour the points were tallied, checked and rechecked. I had finished fourth, a fantastic result.

I joined in the celebrations in a big pit party with beer, barbeques and a big bonfire – the perfect way to end the evening! We crawled back into the apartment at dawn, thankfully with a free day to recover. The cobwebs were blown away with a ride down the Skyline luge run, where a three-wheel cart runs down a concrete track, then got rid of the aches and pains from a hard weekend of racing at a Polynesian spa. Refreshed and rejuvenated, we enjoyed dinner with Frankie and Guy before they flew back to the UK that evening after only four days in New Zealand. Both were due to return less than three weeks later for the Team Championship. You can't fault their commitment, maybe just their sanity!

Lindsey and I now had a few free days to enjoy ourselves. We had a few days in Taupo with Mick Harris and his family, after which we drove the Forgotten World Highway between Taupo and Taranaki. It was like no other road I'd seen before. Lindsey described it as being like Jurassic Park. There are no signs of civilisation; the dirt track winds round hills with huge cliffs on each side, trees have fallen and in some places are nearly blocking the road so you have to get right up to the edge to clear them. The signs say that it is a 100 kilometres per hour speed limit, but in some places we were lucky to manage 10! At the far end of the highway was Graeme Barr's home. I wanted to show my face and help work on the car, although there was little to do. We stayed with Graeme's parents, Trevor and Shirley, and his aunt and uncle returned from holiday with freshly-caught red snapper. The best way to prepare for the next weekend of racing!

The 248 Global Challenge was held in Palmerston North. Once again, I had a practice session. Mick Harris was back racing and he needed the track time since he was racing a different car. I wanted to check the repairs carried out over the week and it was also a chance to familiarise myself with the track. Palmerston North is like a shale version of the Ipswich track, with long straights and big sweeping corners. The start-finish line was nearer the end of the home straight so cars would not be able to pick up as much speed before the first corner as they did at Rotorua and it shouldn't be quite as chaotic. That's what I thought, anyway.

I started the first race on the outside of the second row again. I had a great start but was completely boxed in. I rubbed the back bumper of the car in front but had no-where to go. I was getting bashed from all angles – in New Zealand, the back wheels are enclosed in the sideskids and the front wheels are also well protected, so drivers use the whole car as a weapon. I couldn't force my way to the inside and the momentum of the pack took me side-ways against the wall at the end of the straight. The front end flipped up in the air, a bumper clipped my back end which brought me back down to earth facing the wrong way, then the car was picked up again and swung back round. The rollercoaster came to an end with my car up in the air, balanced on the bonnet of Ricky Logan's car and the wall, leaning at an angle. It was a precarious situation, so red flags were waved and the race halted. It seemed to take an age before they moved the car from underneath me and I got my wheels back down on the track. I asked a marshal if I was good to go, but he said I couldn't because the stoppage was for me. 'You couldn't continue anyway,' he carried on, 'the car doesn't look like it's up to it!'

I didn't even manage half a lap. The car had two burst tyres and damaged rims, another broken shock absorber, a ripped under loop bar, a bent track rod and steering arm, a sideskid bracket was broken off and the gold wing fin was bent and twisted. It took a lot of effort to get it ready for the second race. Kev Smith, a former UK stock car driver with a hard reputation, helped to sort out a lot of the damage. 'Now you see why I don't drive out here,' he told me, 'they're too rough!'

I went out for the second race wanting to give a better account of myself from the middle of the grid. The three-race format means that one non-finish and your championship hopes have gone, but I was aware that many people in New Zealand hadn't seen me before and were probably thinking that this chap from the UK who was calling himself World Champion was a real waste of space. This time I got away safely and when the red flags were waved after a couple of laps it wasn't for me. I finished ninth, finding that my driving style suited the track. The Kiwi drivers raced wide by the wall, screaming the engine in a long broadside sweep round the corners. I took a different line, going a little tighter. They might have looked more spectacular, but I felt that I had more speed without much hassle.

I tried the same again in the third race, which I started from the back of the grid. I immediately made up a few places because Ricky Logan started in front of me and quickly moved out of the way. Ricky is an American sprint car driver who had been racing the sprint season in New Zealand, but he was used to non-contact racing and was bewildered by the brutal superstocks. I nipped up his inside and made progress before the red flags were waved again after a couple of laps. I looked around and found myself amongst Peter Rees, Malcolm Ngatai, Joe Faram and Scott Myers – all drivers in with a good chance of winning the title. My heart has never beaten as forcefully as it did while I was waiting for the green flag to wave. I didn't have a chance of winning the championship and I didn't want to affect the result, but I wanted to prove myself against the best that New Zealand has to offer. I squeezed the steering wheel and focused, again feeling like a soldier waiting to go into battle. I managed to avoid the Kiwi bumpers and finished ninth. Had it not been for a first disappointing race, I would have been up there with the leaders in the overall standings.

My New Zealand adventure had come to an end already. Guy Parker spent the first weekend trying to talk me into staying on an extra two weeks for the Team Championship but I had responsibilities at home. Lindsey was certain that she wanted to return home to see the kids and it wouldn't have been fair to leave them with my parents for longer. I was also aware that a month is a long time to be away from work, especially when it's my own business. Even so, as the time in New Zealand passed, I was increasingly tempted to stay. At one stage I agreed with Lindsey that I would change my flight and stay on for longer.

The plan changed again after hitting the bars in Auckland on the penultimate evening of the trip. The night out ended in the early hours and I woke up the next morning with a bad hangover. If Lindsey went home and Peter Falding came out from the UK for the Team Championship, my level of alcohol intake would increase. Peter would make sure of that! I shouldn't – and couldn't – carry on like that for the next two weeks. Head overruled heart, and I confirmed that I would be flying home as scheduled.

It's a shame that the islands of New Zealand and the UK are so far apart because the experience of racing out there is fantastic. The Kiwis are friendly and welcoming to their stock car brethren from the UK and we were well looked after by everybody we encountered. The scenery is wonderful and the lifestyle is very relaxing and laid back. Yet I couldn't live there. I like people and crowds. New Zealand has roughly about the same land area as the UK, but only 4 million people as opposed to 60 million. Still, it is an amazing place to visit, and hopefully it won't be another seventeen years before I'm back.

Can you tell that I'm cold, wet and miserable?

9

A new season, a new start. Only it didn't start so well for me.

After such a cracking season, winning the World Final, British Championship and a World Semi-Final, I should have been on a high. I should have felt confident and buzzing, ready to take on all-comers as the World Champion. Instead, I felt as though I'd got to the top of the mountain. The view was great, but from the top of the mountain there is only one way. And that's down.

My first appearance was on Good Friday at Skegness. It wasn't a World Championship qualifier, but it was the track that the World Final would be run on. It was a good opportunity to give the tarmac car a shakedown.

There hadn't been a huge amount of work done on the car over the winter, it was just a case of taking out the engine and putting in a replacement. The new engine came with the Chris Walker car that I bought in 2005, since then it had been sat under a bench in the workshop for a few years. Deciding that a fresh engine would do the tarmac car some good, I sent the old Walker engine for a rebuild by Andy Maynard at Hi-Spec. We had a little bit of work to make the engine fit once it came back and there was a little bit of bumper work here and there, but the car was ready for the new season in plenty of time.

It was a typical early April day – cold, damp and drizzling. We went out for the first heat with one of last year's part-worn tyres on; for the second heat I tried shale tyres. The shale ones didn't work too well, so I went back to the part-worn ones for the final and Grand National. My results improved throughout the evening – seventh in Heat 1, fifth in the final and fourth in the Grand National – maybe because I was getting used to racing again after the winter layoff. However, I couldn't help but notice that other drivers were throwing new rubber on their cars like it was a major championship. Tom Harris came away with three race wins, but he must have spent as much money on new tyres as he earned from the victories. Danny Wainman had a brand new tyre on his outside rear wheel for one of the heats which he also used in the final, then put on another brand new tyre for the Grand National. Lee Fairhurst and Mick Sworder also had good meetings, but how much was down to them and how much was down to the amount they were spending on tyres? They are all enthusiastic drivers who were keen to come out of the traps really quickly at the start of the season, stamping their mark and laying down a gauntlet to their rivals.

The following day at Coventry I was reunited with my shale car. We had not done much with it over the course of the previous season, and while it could still be very quick in the right conditions, it was beginning to get a bit tatty. Tom Harris took it away for a refurbishment, freshening up the chassis and structure, while the engine also went away to Hi-Spec. Tom brought it to Coventry for me, the first time I'd seen the car since he took it away at the end of last season.

It was cold and damp again. The car was pushing into corners terribly, turning too late, which was typical of the shale car in poor conditions. I struggled all meeting to take the push out of the car, but no matter what I did and what I altered, it didn't seem to make any difference. The brakes were not right either, Tom had altered the engine mounting plates so it sat more rigidly, the same as the tarmac car, but part of the structure alteration meant that I wasn't getting full travel on the brake pedal. Normally I would stamp on the brake pedal and throw the car into the corner, but now I couldn't do that. Two fifth places were the unspectacular result.

I didn't exactly hit the ground running. I had already missed the first meeting of the season, at Belle Vue, because it was Lindsey's 40th birthday. We went to Bruges with family and friends for a sightseeing and drinking weekend. The following weekend, a King's Lynn meeting, it was my daughter Melissa's birthday. I passed on the racing again in favour of going to Alton Towers. Over the Easter weekend, I chose to miss Monday's Belle Vue in favour of a few days in Norfolk and another birthday party.

To be honest, I started on a bit of a low. Racing wasn't a priority. I had lost a little bit of my mojo.

I wanted to give a good account of myself with the gold roof. However, I wasn't prepared to break the bank to do it. I had hoped that winning the World Final would encourage a major sponsor to get on board, but that didn't happen. I decided that I wouldn't feel obliged to race in meetings just because I was the World Champion.

In previous years I've looked forward to the World Final – that has been my one target for the season. I would look at the fixture list and plan my route there, all the time wondering – is this my year? I wasn't sure how it would affect me now that I had won it. Maybe that dented my motivation a little.

I was also aware that there was a gap alongside me at the back of the grid. Andy Smith's retirement was a shame for the sport, but stock car racing is bigger than any one driver or family. His dad retired, my dad retired, Frankie Wainman Senior retired, but each time the sport continued. There is plenty of new blood coming through the sport that will take Andy's place. The likes of Tom Harris, Mat Newson, Dan Johnson and Lee Fairhurst will take the sport into 2020 and beyond.

Stock car racing would survive, but would I? Andy's retirement made me question my own future. It felt like the end of my stock car racing career was coming. Seeing some of my mates like Peter Falding and Andy Smith drop out, guys who I knocked around with when we were just kids, I was beginning to feel like the last man standing. It felt as though my retirement was just round the corner.

I needed to shake myself out of it. I had two fresh cars, now I needed a fresh head. Next up was a tarmac weekend, Birmingham and Hednesford, both World Championship qualifiers. Tom Harris and Frankie Wainman Junior sat at the top of the qualifying chart, already looking like safe bets to take pole position in the two semi-finals. I had my eye on fifth or sixth position. That would put me on the inside of the second row in one of the semi-finals.

Looking for a bit of a kick-start, I bought a new off-side rear tyre. That tyre was used in the heats and finals at both meetings, each time switching to an older tyre for the Grand National. It gave me the little boost I was looking for. I felt as quick as anyone else around me all weekend, whether or not they had brand new rubber on. In my best result of the weekend, third place in the final at Hednesford, the only two drivers who beat me were Lee Fairhurst and Stuart Smith Junior, both of whom went from the front of the reds. It was a good weekend. The tarmac car felt more on the pace than it had during its previous run out at Skegness and I thought that there was still more to come from it. Perhaps more importantly, I felt that I had blown the cobwebs away and was racing with more enthusiasm and commitment.

Tarmac car sorted, now it was time to get the shale car up to scratch. Two double-meeting shale weekends were coming up, taking in the four major shale tracks. The first meeting was at King's Lynn. On track in the first heat, it seemed the shale car had matched the tarmac car's improvement. While it was damp, the track had a good slick line and it felt like the conditions were just right for my car. I finished in third, well ahead of the other stars and superstars, with only Paul Spooner and Russell Cooper in front.

I should have been in a good mood, but I was already riled. Ministox were supporting the bill and Bradley had gone on track in the first heat. There are certain things that you can do on track and certain things that you should not. What I have told Bradley not to do, even showing him clips on YouTube, is exactly what he did. Just as he was challenging for the top spots at the end of the race, he went into a corner and got up the inside of the car that was in front of him. He tried a trick that many drivers often play both in Ministox and in other stock car formulae – he squeezed the other driver to the outside towards the fence as they drove down the straight. By all means lean on them coming out of the corner until you get to a point where you are level with them, but at that point you must start turning away from them. If you keep pushing them towards the fence you leave your back-end vulnerable if they cut back across and the result can be a spin or even a rollover. That's exactly what happened to Bradley, and he went on his roof for the first time in his racing career. It wasn't a dirty move, it was a sloppy one, but he went from a race-winning opportunity to a messy car.

While Bradley was getting a mouthful from me, the rest of the team were looking at my car. The engine was flooding up and I didn't make it out for the next heat, and by the time the final came around the heavens had opened. There was no chance of a good slick line now, it would be more like driving in one of the East Anglian fields, so I opted for something not tried before. We put a rally tyre on the offside front, hoping to gain extra grip through the corners. It didn't work. Straight away I could tell that the car did not want to turn and it pushed on into the corners. I managed to struggle through to third or fourth in the final by the time the yellow flags were waved, bringing the race to a temporary stop. On the restart, Tom Harris caught me going into the turn, exaggerating the push, and I clattered into the back of Paul Hines who was parked in the fence. I had to back up and lost a lap, eventually getting ninth place.

We switched the useless rally tyre for a Goodyear in the Grand National and it made a real difference. I was travelling well, but then near the end of the race Mick Sworder went into a corner a little heavily and clipped a car up against the fence, spinning him around straight into my path. I hit him hard, head-on, and it knocked the wind out of my sails. Like before, I struggled on to claim fifth place, but it could have been much better.

We chugged up across the country to Belle Vue the following day, but the weather was no better. All across the Woodhead Pass it was chucking it down and it was still coming down as we pulled into the pits. One of my mechanics looked through the window and said, 'if we turn around and head back now, we can be in Rotherham in time to have Sunday lunch in a pub before Heat 1 starts.' With that in my mind, straight away my chin was on the floor. I got wrapped up in waterproofs, the hood was tied tightly round my face, I also had a balaclava on underneath. We were dodging puddles in the pits so the track was likely to be a quagmire. It wouldn't suit my shale car, which is better when the track dries out a little. What was I doing here? It was raining and blooming freezing.

My attitude was all wrong. I was interviewed by Premier Sports and I said some things I shouldn't have: I was downbeat about the weather and the meeting, and I basically called it as I felt at the time – I didn't want to be there. It wasn't very befitting of the World Champion. If I really felt like that, I should have stayed at home.

Bradley still wasn't out of the firing line either. 'Look at that! You've bent it,' I said, pointing at the front of his

Ministox chassis. 'You've messed your car now, it'll never be as good again!'

Bradley was giving as good as he got. 'There's nothing wrong with it! It was like that before!'

'If you listened to me more, it would show in your results!'

Bradley must have gone out on track with my bollocking ringing in his ears but then he went and won the first race. I wasn't sure whether to be pleased that he'd won or annoyed that he'd proved me wrong.

I went out in my first heat and because I expected the track to be a little boggy, I opted for an old Weathermaster tyre on the offside rear. It comes out once in a blue moon when conditions are at their worst, but it was evident after the first or second lap that I was over-tyred. The rain had stopped and the track was in better shape than I expected – I'd made the wrong call. I was struggling, nearly getting lapped by the leaders, when James Morris climbed over my sideskid and knocked my shock absorber off. I crawled onto the infield, but without the shocker my car was like a snowplough. The sump stuck in the mud and dragged along, scraping half the infield onto it which turned into a massive task to clear out. The bottom pulley and power steering pump were both hidden and totally clogged by all the mud. In the second heat, with the right tyre on, the car was better. I still wasn't really up for it though, and although I got sixth place, it felt like I wasn't in the same race as the five who finished in front of me. I needed to get a higher temperature in the inside rear tyre, but when I pulled off the track at the end of the race the rubber was still rock hard.

By the time the final came round, the track started to slick up properly. For the last few laps of the race, as conditions turned in my favour, the car started to speed up. I caught up to Rob Speak, who was making a (supposedly) one-off appearance for charity and wasn't in the mood to take any prisoners. Any cars that tried to get past him, or any cars that Rob caught up, were stuffed in the fence for fun. The way I'd been driving, I didn't feel taking Rob on was the right thing to do. Mark Gilbank was a fair distance behind me, so I sat behind Rob until the last corner. I saved a little bump for him, just enough to put him out wide into the mud, and took fourth place. Though feeling a bit happier, I didn't bother to go out for the Grand National. It's very rare that I load up early through choice, but I decided that I was so frustrated that it would be better to save the car for the following weekend. I knew that I was capable of much better. I doubt the spectators will have even noticed whether I was at the meeting or not.

Maybe something in my subconscious told me that the weather and conditions didn't suit my car, so I didn't bother to apply myself 100%. Or maybe it was part of the bigger picture. Andy's retirement, the amount being spent on tyres, Bradley's rollover, the weather – it all contributed to making me feel a bit down, and the results reflected that. I needed something to spark my enthusiasm for stock cars again.

Following Dad at the launch of *The Harrison Dynasty*

10

As so often happens, it was my dad who helped get me out of it.

Between us, we've been involved in stock cars every season since the sport started in 1954. Racing was Dad's life. I was born on Good Friday in 1969. Things were a little different back then and fathers weren't present at the birth, but they usually hung around somewhere nearby. In my case, I think the hospital staff and other patients felt sorry for my mum because they thought she was a single parent. Dad popped in on Friday, then on Saturday he was off racing at Nelson, Sunday at Brands Hatch and Monday at Belle Vue!

Keith Barber approached me sometime close to the last World Final saying that he wanted to write a book. What he wanted was to publish my dad's story, he has more history in the sport than anybody else who is still involved. There are a lot of people who want to hear about it and Dad is quite happy to share his tales with anyone who will listen. So I didn't hesitate and told Keith straight away that I thought it was a great idea. So many people go through life with an amazing story and never get the chance to tell it; it was an opportunity not to be missed. I spoke with Keith many times on the telephone, he also talked to my dad and came up from Cornwall to spend some time with him and look over his photo collection.

There was a special meeting at Coventry to mark the launch. We hadn't seen the book in any form before we arrived at the stadium, in fact the first time I saw it was when a person passed it to me asking for an autograph. Keith also brought along my dad's car that he raced from 1966 to 1970, painted up in the colours that my dad used. We parked my car and Bradley's Ministox next to it so the spectators could see the three generations of cars, and the three generations of drivers sat under a gazebo signing books. It was a great event for my dad – Bradley and I are just a passing chapter of it as far as I'm concerned.

When the time came around to go out on track, the three of us were asked to drive round in our cars. I was a little anxious. Keith told my dad that the steering was heavy and I didn't want him to get in there, overexert himself and pull a muscle or lose control and run into the fence – he's 74 and hasn't been in a stock car for a number of years after all – but I needn't have worried. He sat down, pressed the clutch, started the engine, put it in gear and drove away like he had never stopped racing. The idea was that we would do couple of slow laps waving at the crowd, but once we got on track Dad floored it and he was pulling away from me – I had to change into top gear to keep up with him! Dad wears a peaked fisherman's cap at stock car meetings to keep the wind and the rain off his head. He said that he wanted to go faster but his hat was already threatening to blow off so he was trying to hold it on with one hand! With hindsight we could have put a crash helmet on and fastened him in with a harness so he could have put on a really good show, but as it was he thoroughly enjoyed the occasion and I was pleased that people made a fuss of him.

It was back to proper racing after that, but with a more positive head fixed on. I had a bit of time to get ready and went out in the last heat, but I was struggling with the car a little bit. Craig Finnikin, Mick Sworder, Dave Willis and Murray Harrison got away from me, but I had the best seat in the house to watch their battle. Moving into the final, I still found that the track was too damp for my car. It came good in the last few laps when the shale moved off the racing line, but only in time for me to pick up a lowly place. We altered a few things for the Grand National and I was quicker, getting back up to fourth place. It was no coincidence that it was towards the end of a meeting, when the shale is slicker, that I felt I was having my best drives.

Perhaps my best achievement at the following meeting in Sheffield was that I could load up at the end of the meeting with four races, four finishes and no damage. The same couldn't be said for Mark Gilbank, who hit James Morris and Scott Davids after James lost control and bounced out of the fence. Mark took a lot of damage and had to retire from the meeting after the first race. I was lucky – I ran over the wheel and half shaft that came out of Scott's car in the same crash, but didn't take any damage and finished in fourth. For the second heat we tinkered a little with the settings and I was right on the pace, getting second place behind Neil Shenton. It was my best result of the season so far, and had I not been in the race with Neil, a Sheffield track specialist who was undergraded at yellow, I'd probably have won by a mile.

Both the final and Grand National were unspectacular affairs. I avoided incidents and accidents, driving smoothly and circulating at a reasonable pace. Fifth, second, fourth and seventh were reasonable results at a dangerous track, and they were all World Championship qualifying points that were helping keep me in a good position for my favoured fifth or sixth place in the standings. Not a bad day at the office.

It was back to the Skegness tarmac for the following weekend, and I was feeling better about it. The tarmac car had been pretty good in its three meetings so far, there hadn't been any meetings where I felt too far from the pace. There was only one thing holding me back: tyres.

At every meeting so far, whether tarmac or shale, some drivers had been throwing two or three new tyres on the car. The first time a new tyre is raced on the outside rear wheel it helps improve performance, and a lot of drivers were trying to gain an advantage in as many races as possible by putting on a brand new tyre. I had been racing on part-worn older tyres which still raced well for five races or so but did not have the immediate impact of that crucial first use. Having new rubber every time makes the racing very expensive, but you needed it if you wanted to compete on a level playing field with the other star drivers.

Realising that there was a risk that some drivers would be priced out, the BSCDA introduced a new tyre rule for tarmac meetings. Now, a tyre used on the outside rear wheel in a meeting final or Grand National had to be used in two other races first. It meant that drivers couldn't keep throwing a new tyre on every time they race in a final or Grand National and all drivers would use fewer tyres on the whole.

More importantly for me, I felt it would make a significant difference to my own results. Instead of going out on track with a part-worn tyre while others had a new tyre on the outside rear, giving them an immediate performance advantage, now they would also have to use part-worn tyres. I felt that my tarmac car had been on the pace so far even with the detrimental tyres, now it could perform on a level playing field.

Maybe I would even have an advantage. I was used to racing part-worn tyres, whereas a lot of the other drivers who used new rubber all the time might suffer a little bit. I knew that I could preserve tyres, keeping it fairly smooth and not getting overexcited on track. Could the younger drivers, smoking tyres in and out of corners with their committed full-on driving style, hold the performance of the tyres for so long?

What was clear was that this could be a turning point. I knew that I hadn't carried the gold roof as well as I'd hoped for the first quarter of the season. Now, with important races on the horizon, circumstances were beginning to turn in my favour.

I always look forward to the Skegness UK Open weekend. It's a good place to race; I enjoy the track, you need to think a lot round Skegness, you can't just get your head down and go all guns blazing. And there was an extra spice in the air this year as drivers would be trying to work out the best setup for the World Final.

Straight away I felt like I was one of the quickest on track and the car was well on the pace. In the first race, I made it up to third place with one lap to go. I had a dive at Mat Newson on the last bend but couldn't get past, we crossed the line one after the other: Rob Cowley, Mat Newson, then me. Unfortunately, Bradley's racing weekend didn't start as well. It was over after his second race, a couple of pistons were breaking up in his engine. It was too much to try and fix in the pits, so his Ministox was loaded back up and he would be a spectator for the rest of the weekend. He was among the good-size crowd watching me in the final, which was a fantastic race. I was in the pack and there were big hits going in on every single corner. The superstars were trading big blows, each looking to break free.

However, as I was driving down the straight it all went wrong. The nose cone appeared to have been badly worn and the spigot pilot bearing, on the front shaft of the gearbox where it goes into the back of the crank, had broken up. It affected the clutch, ripping the splines out of the outer and inner clutch plates and ripping the centre out of the inner clutch plate – basically, the clutch had gone. I didn't know this when I went down the straight. I just knew there was a clatter and bang and the drive had gone. Sat on the infield, I wondered whether it was the differential, the gearbox or the clutch. When I got back to the pits, we quickly saw that it was the clutch. The spigot pilot bearing that had broken up was difficult to get out and we soon realised I wasn't going to make it for the Grand National.

Skegness weekenders are not just about the racing, and it was the early hours when I got into bed after making use of the bar with the Dutch racers and fans who had come across for the weekend. The next morning I rose late, but the crew, with help from Andy Maynard who built the engine, had got on with it and got the pilot bearing out. They had to borrow a tool from Mat Newson to grind it out and it collapsed on itself. Although it was a pain to fix, we were lucky that the damage wasn't too bad. Out of all the possible problems, it was the cheapest thing to repair. When I emerged from the bus at 11:30, just as the crew were finishing off (and I appreciate everything you do, guys!) my priority was to find Chris Binns. He had done a painting of my car, my dad's car and Bradley's car, all with a gold roof, for my dad's 75th birthday that morning. My aim was to win the UK Open Championship for him later that day.

In no time I had to be out for my heat. The car was sound again, the damage from the previous day had been fixed and it wasn't carrying any other minor damage. With the new tyre rule coming into effect, drivers had to run new tyres during the heats to get two stamps on them ready for the final, when we must use a two-race old tyre. I used one new tyre during Saturday's heat and then again in the first heat on Sunday, then used one of last year's old tyres in the second heat. Considering it was an old tyre, the car felt really good and on the pace. I got past Mick Sworder and Dan Johnson easily enough but got caught up with a couple of blues who weren't travelling as fast. That gave Dan an opportunity to fire Mick at me and come back past, so I had to squabble my way back past them both again. I ended up in fourth – the same result as in the first heat – and on the strength of those two results I was the best-scoring superstar, so I would start from the front of the superstars in the UK Open final.

I was up for it and confident. It was the first time I was on track with everybody else around me using an offside rear tyre which was at least two races old. Now we were even.

I was involved in an early battle with the superstars, with Frankie, Tom Harris and Mick Sworder in particular. I got a bump early on that allowed a couple of cars to pass me, but then I clawed my way to the front of the superstar pack again. I could see in my mirrors that Mick was behind me. He would have seen that I was travelling fast. At that point, if I were in Mick's position, I would have settled in behind me to break away from the other superstars. His priority should have been to catch the fast low-graders then deal with me at the end of the race. Instead, Mick took huge lunges at me, trying to get past every corner. It slowed me down, but it slowed him down as well. The other superstars could keep in touch with us and ultimately it just meant that we were racing for the lower places.

In contrast, a race where two drivers used their heads to get a good result was my last big race at Skegness, the World Semi-Final. Frankie was clever enough to settle behind me early on in the race. He realised he could either take second place and have a chance for first place in the last couple of laps if he wanted it, or he could clatter me early on in the race, but that would risk both of us fighting for fourth and fifth at the end. I think we both appreciated the other's tactics at the end of that one.

Back at the UK Open, there was one bend where Mick took a big pot shot at me. He had to go over the kerb sideways to hit me and it sent me over to the pit gate which allowed Frankie to get between us. It was a suicide dive, and so early on in the race it was futile. The following corner I was pushed wide by Frankie, who was obviously keen to take his chance to get past us. I recovered and got away from Mick and Frankie, and by the end of the race I was catching the first four. Had Mick not taken me out earlier in the race, I might have been up there on the podium, even with a win. More importantly from Mick's point of view, he might have been up there with me.

There's no doubt that Mick is a good driver and a fantastic one for the spectators to watch. His driving style is sometimes worth the entrance money alone, similar to Andy Smith's in some ways, but he can be frustrating to race against. It's good to be involved in a race with him, but he makes moves that I would not have chosen, moves that delay the race of the superstar pack as a whole. Treating every corner like it's the last bend allows the fast lower-graders to get away and stops the back of the grid getting forward as a hunting pack. Often it means that the superstars are racing for the minor places rather than racing for first.

The drivers who finished in front of me were Rob Cowley who started from yellow, Luke Davidson from blue, and Stuart Smith Junior from red. All of them started from an advantageous grade and were soon to be upgraded. Wesley Schaap also started from yellow; he is a talented driver, just starting out, and had the benefit of using Ron Kroonder's car. Considering that, I was really pleased with fifth place and clearly being the top superstar.

The new tyre rule seemed to have had a positive impact in its first meeting. Now I just need to wait for them to introduce the same rule on shale.

I suppose I could clean my helmet and goggles a little
more often!

11

My sister's birthday is always around the same time as the Northampton and Buxton World Championship qualifiers, so I usually miss any celebrations. This year was a little different. I'd won the World Final, which meant that the qualifiers were now a little less important, and it was my sister's 40th. I told her to count me in this year.

Eighteen people were booked in for a trip to Playa Las Americas in Tenerife. My sister lives in Essex, so I picked up a couple of friends at Newark and banged down the A1. It was about 9 o'clock at night, the roads were quiet, and unfortunately I got pulled for speeding. I had my foot down when my mate in the back seat leaned forward and said, 'did you see that police car on the bridge we've just passed?' Sure enough, blue lights appeared behind me a couple of minutes later. The officer got me in the back of the car and said, 'do you know how fast you were travelling?' I hoped that he'd got me at a decent level, so shrugged and said, 'about 80?' When he showed me his speed gun, it showed 95mph. I was distraught. It was the first time I had been pulled over for speeding since I was 18. I was ultra-humble in the back of the car, asking for the benefit of the doubt, but he replied, 'you get the benefit of the doubt up to a certain level, but at 95 you're fairly close to having to go to court to get a bigger fine and more points.' It was a fair cop. My mates in the car told me I should have played the celebrity card. I don't think that would have worked, although ticketing a world champion racing driver would have been a great story for his mates at the station!

Once in the more relaxed surroundings of our all-inclusive hotel in Tenerife, we camped out round the swimming pool, chilling out and having a beer. We played plenty of games around the pool. A killer darts game started with around twenty people and finished with a tense duel between the last two: me and Andy Smith! Naturally, I beat him, but it was very competitive for a time. Everybody else had retired back to the pool saying, 'lads, it's just a game of darts,' but we didn't see it that way. When a victorious Harrison and stroppy Smith got back to the sun loungers afterwards, I gently took the piss out of him. He said, 'you'll not be laughing when I get home. I'm going to get on the phone and order a load of steel so I can build a new stock car, then I'll take you out on the track!' So if Andy does come out of retirement, you'll have me to thank for it!

I'd missed a weekend of racing, but there was still plenty to come. Each year, there is a stage of the season when drivers need to start turning in good results to show people that they are there or thereabouts for the major championships. I knew I needed to build on the UK Open weekend and start making an impression on the races that mattered.

I went to the King's Lynn weekender feeling positive. I'd been saying for months that I thought cold, damp tracks were affecting my car. Now it was the time of year that weather conditions would be changing to suit my car for the better. However, right from the first heat the car wasn't quick enough. It wasn't bad for any particular reason, but last year when the track was drying out I had an edge, especially later on in a race. That wasn't happening this time. I spent the whole of the Saturday meeting looking for why that was and I couldn't put my finger on it. During the Grand National I felt a vibration at the top end of the revs, so after the meeting we got the car back in the pits and stripped it down, looking for what it might be. It might be the differential, but we checked it and found no problem. We took out the gearbox and checked it too, but there was nothing obvious. Just in case, it was sent over to Murray Harrison who stripped it overnight. We checked the clutch, mainly because we'd had a problem with the clutch at Skegness. Although it was a different car, it seemed worthwhile looking at. We checked the bearings on the back axle, no problems there either.

When we got the prop shaft off, we thought there might be a little bit of play in it, but I was doubtful that it was significant enough to affect the car and to create the vibration. Mike Williamson was parked next to us in the pits and had a new prop shaft, and he let us take it. We put everything back together for Sunday morning and it seemed to have solved the problem. No vibration.

The track conditions were perfect for my car, it was dry and sunny. It should have been a great meeting. However, in the first heat I got in a dogfight with half a dozen drivers and finished up somewhere in the lower places. I came off feeling really disillusioned. The car was still not performing as well as it should in the conditions. The team put it down to the rear outside tyre, that I was being too tight and not putting a new tyre on often enough, so we put a better tyre on for the final. Suddenly I was flying, battling with Craig Finnikin at the front of the other reds and superstars, when I got a flat. Then in the Grand National, the car again felt mint. I went into a corner and finished up in a bit of a melee with Paul Hines. I bent my panhard rod and I had to pull off, but I was heartened that the car had handled a lot better just for the sake of a better tyre.

Unfortunately, that was the difference. Chuck a better tyre at the car on the rear outside and it would go faster. I was just trying to make tyres last too long, but the car wouldn't have it and I couldn't match the other quick guys. I was frustrated because I didn't want to keep spending, but the difference between running a new tyre and one that's three or four races old is between finishing in the first four and just finishing in the top ten. King's Lynn was a wake-up call that I had to spend a bit more money on tyres. I had come to the same decision last year but much earlier in the season. Over the winter I slipped back into my old ways and it had taken me too long to get out of it. The lads in the garage are not quick to point that out to me and slam it in my face. They know it is a cost issue and they know that I am aware of the situation. They leave me to play with my own demons in my head.

So we went to Coventry the following weekend with better rubber on. In my heat the car felt good, then I went out in the final with a brand new tyre on. It was a good race, a proper stock car battle, and I was mixing it with the best of them. I got in a bit of a ruck that cost me a little time but towards the end of the race I was coming on really strong. With about four laps to go there was a pile-up mid-corner at the end of the back straight, just as I had got on Frankie's back bumper. I was concentrating solely on him. Normally I would read a race, seeing what is afoot in front, but here I was just concentrating on Frankie for a minute. Because I took my eye off the rest of the race, I didn't see the melee and ended up following Frankie round the outside of the pile-up. Had I been looking further ahead, I could have gone on the inside, overtaking Frankie as I did so. Nonetheless, I was convinced that the car was much improved and my thoughts about the effects of running a better tyre were confirmed. I left the new tyre on and went out for the Grand National, but the conditions suddenly changed. It belted down.

I sat on the grid thinking the track would be really bad. Should I just pull off and not bother? I didn't want to waste the new tyre, I didn't want to damage the car, I didn't want to get it six inches deep in shite, I was going straight from the meeting to Norfolk for a holiday, I didn't want to get crapped up. It was a fleeting moment in my mind, but when the green flag fell it was put to the back of my head. I took the race slow and steady, knowing that some drivers would try to win it on the first lap, but when the track is wet and slippery you have to stay in control. While I watched other drivers spinning off and going out wide in the crap, I did not put a wheel on the loose shale. There was a stoppage and I looked around and found myself in a reasonable position. Will Yarrow and Tom Harris were in front of me. On the restart I got past Tom, then there was another stoppage. I maintained position on the green flag. Will was driving well, but there was a car parked up on the kerb on the first corner which forced him wider than he would have wanted to go and he slipped on the loose shale. That gave me a chance and I got round the inside and into the lead. I was looking in my mirror constantly. I wanted to back off because the muck screen had come adrift and the radiator had more shale in it than it would normally have, so the engine was getting warmer than I would have liked. But there was a car continually pushing behind me – I didn't realise at the time it was Will because of the shale plastered all over it – and I had to keep far enough in front of him that he couldn't make contact with my back bumper. I kept on the racing line and far enough away from him that the chequered flag was waved and I recorded my first race win of the season. It was a bit dismal that it had taken so long when I was World Champion, but I was nonetheless pleased.

I missed the tarmac weekend at Birmingham and Northampton. Neither of them were qualifiers, so I went to a full weekend Skegness meeting with Bradley and his Ministox. It was a lot cheaper travelling to Skegness, just needing a couple of gallons of petrol for the Mini and one trip in the bus rather than a couple of drives to different tracks and all the running costs associated with my Formula 1. It was a good social weekend with no pressure and I was prepared to sacrifice my weekend for Bradley to enjoy his last year of racing Ministox. That he got plenty of places and a couple of race wins made it even better.

It gave me some thinking time too. I had run out of excuses. The weather was better, meaning that my car should be at its best. I was spending more money on better tyres. There was just one other piece of the jigsaw. Myself. The meetings at King's Lynn and Coventry were the first ones of the season where I could honestly say I had put in a distinct effort. Better weather and tyres matched with better attitude equalled better performances. It showed that you have got to have the right mental attitude in stock cars. If you turn up with the wrong attitude – as I had done a few times this season – you might as well stay at home. It's a waste of time. I'd made progress over the last couple of meetings, but I needed to stay on top of my game and not let the focus and determination drop.

There were only two more weekends of World Championship qualifiers, at Buxton and Ipswich. I'm not fanatical about Buxton. Without big grids it can become a little bit of a drag, although I'd won the final last time I raced there. There are two long straights and a couple of tight corners, so we put a different set of gearing in the car. I went out for the first heat but immediately I was struggling for revs off the corners. We got it wrong, I was a gear set too high. I was also juggling the tyres and didn't put on a brand new tyre for the heat like some of the other drivers did. The end result was sixth. In the second heat, I was definitely better with a more appropriate gear ratio and got fifth. Then with better tyres for the final, I felt like I stood a chance. We also changed the inside front brake pad, one of the mechanics had noted that it was a little bit worn and you really need good brakes at Buxton. I had a short drive around the pits with my foot on the brake to try and warm them up and get a heat cycle through them.

I started from the inside of the second row of the superstars. I went past a couple on the first lap and settled in just behind Lee Fairhurst, although not on his back bumper. That was a mistake, because on the second lap I found myself on the front of a train of superstars with no cushion in front of me. I was the front car, and as everybody rattled into the back of each other I catapulted off the front and hit the fence hard sideways. There was no significant damage to the steering so I carried on, but as I got to the end of the next straight I realised I had lost the brakes. There was damage to the offside front caliper, so I retired to the centre green and watched Will Yarrow drive well to win, holding off Tom Harris for the last three laps. When I got back in the pits I realised that there was even more damage. The impact had broken the cross on the front of the chassis, the panhard rod was bent and the axle was bent. We cobbled the car back together and put a different caliper on, but there was only one race between the final and the Grand National and little could be done about the broken cross. The axle wasn't perfect and the wheel rim was still buckled. I nursed it home for sixth because it was a qualifying round, but when I came off after the race there was still a lot that needed attention.

I had a decision to make. Did I go to Ipswich the next weekend? The results at Buxton meant that Mat Newson had leapfrogged me and pushed me down to seventh. In an ideal world, I wanted fifth or sixth, that would get me a slot on the inside of the second row of a semi-final. To achieve that, I needed to go to Ipswich. I knew that Dan Johnson wasn't attending, so I only needed about three or four points, something which I should easily get barring a disaster. I thought seriously about it, but it was a 390-mile round trip, about £300 of diesel and a new tyre. We would have to change the gears again and get the car patched up. While loading up, we also noticed that the fuel tank was leaking. It would involve a lot of work to get it ready for the next weekend. I decided to give Ipswich a miss.

I presumed that my outside second-row start would be at King's Lynn because it was fairly obvious that the top scorer, Tom Harris, would choose the Birmingham semi-final. I didn't see that starting on the outside at King's Lynn was a huge problem. I started there in the World Final in 2007 and had a good race, eventually finishing in fourth.

And there was another factor that affected my decision not to race at Ipswich – I had a new car to sort out.

A month earlier at King's Lynn, Geritt Zwerver, the Dutchman who owns the racing tracks at Blauwhuis, came over for a chat with John Schaap, the brother of Dave. They had noticed that I had 'sponsors required' on the side of my car. So far nothing fruitful had come of it, but we got chatting about a potential deal. I'd heard that he bought the occasional British stock car to take to Holland and was aware that the big-block engined shale car that I used in the Belle Vue Shootout finale would be a good buy for him. It has an LD back axle which they prefer in Holland because they are more withstanding on the bumpy tracks. We arranged that in a couple of weeks, the next time he was coming across the channel to pick up a car from Frankie, he would come and have a look at it. That happened in the week between Buxton and Ipswich and he chose to buy it. Part of the package we agreed was that I would put the name of his website, stockcarmak-elaar.nl, on my cars.

Within a couple of hours, and not knowing anything about the sale, one of the lads who works for me said, 'have you seen Dave Riley's car is for sale on the internet?'

'What, the one that Tom has just built? That's a nice car!' I replied. The cogs in my mind immediately started to turn. I retreated to my office and had a look at it online. After this season, the next two World Finals would definitely be on shale, and there is a chance that one or two after that might be as well. The car that Dave was selling was only five meetings old and it looked like no expense had been spared on it. The only reason that Dave was getting rid of it was so he could concentrate on single-surface racing; he much prefers tarmac.

The Riley car was a big step up from what I had been racing. My car had a design that was about 20 years old, a Transit front axle on single arms and an LD back axle on single trailing arms with a third link in the boot. It was a bog-standard design two decades ago, and things have developed over the years. A lot of cars now have four-link suspensions on front and back with a Transit back axle so you can alter the weight in the car as you want it. My brakes were old-fashioned, nowadays many drivers have bigger brakes more suited to the way that we race. Dave's car also had left-foot braking which I had got on with quite well in New Zealand.

I decided it would be a good idea to have an upgrade. I wanted to keep my current engine and gearbox and transfer it to the Riley car because it had been revamped over the winter. My shale car could then take the place of the big-block car I'd just got rid of and be stored in a container. I even had a spare engine, the one that won the World Final last year, which could go in it. That car was originally a tarmac car and still had all the brackets for it to be quickly converted back to tarmac racing, so it would be a useful dual-surface car either for me to use as a reserve or potentially for Bradley if he wants to race in the next year or so.

I rang Dave and asked if he would consider splitting the car because he was selling it with engine and gearbox. We did a deal and I arranged for the car to be picked up by one of Tom Harris's men. He brought it to me so I could have a quick sit in it to check the size and decide on any alterations, then took the car away together with my engine and gearbox so Tom could put it all together. Dave had run the car with a big-block engine so it would need some alterations to accommodate my small-block. There were two big shale meetings coming up, the British Championship and the semi-final at King's Lynn. I considered racing my current car in those before switching to the new one – better the devil you know – but I also hoped that the new car would gain me an immediate advantage, that it would be a quicker car straight out of the box. What was the point in waiting? Get on with it and jump in at the deep end!

Luckily we had another weekend of tarmac racing at Skegness so Tom had time to get the new shale car ready. It was a weekend primarily for Formula 2 and saloons, so a lot of drivers took the opportunity to have a weekend off in preparation for the run of big meetings that followed. It meant that a recent trend in tarmac racing was made even more apparent – the increasing domination of lower-graded drivers.

It was something that I'd noticed at Buxton, when Nigel Harrhy won two races without passing a single car. Then, over the course of the Skegness weekend, not a single race was won by a red top. With few cars on the track, the drivers at the front had very few problems and could get away from the chasers with ease. They all had good cars; looking around the pits many white tops had cars that compared with those at the back of the grid. Mark Allen's car was an up-to-date Tom Harris model with an all-singing, all-dancing engine in it. Dave Riley had a lovely tarmac car that was of-the-moment. Mickey Randall had a great machine, and Nigel Harrhy was driving Andy Smith's old car. At the time I thought he was crazy to buy it – he could have had a car designed around him and his own specifications and built by Frankie for less than what he paid – but the car was certainly helping him to good results from the front of the grid.

When these drivers got away, they were not squabbling with each other. None of them were bumper men, they all had good tackle and they all drive good laps. You could put one of the superstars in their car and they wouldn't be that much quicker. The races were like practice laps for them, it was drag racing. They weren't really stock car racing because they weren't having to pass cars, they were just concentrating on nice tidy lines and going as fast as they could.

What the guys at the back needed (and maybe the fans too) were incidents and accidents on the track that slowed everybody up and boxed them together. However, everybody having fast cars of similar spec with equally good drivers in them meant that nobody was held up, there were no incidents and accidents, and the quick lads at the back didn't get the opportunity to use a bit of a racecraft to get on.

My car was good at the Skegness weekend, but I spent all race scrapping to get away from the reds, never getting a chance to get close to the front. In the heats on the first day I didn't have the best tyres on – that problem again of not having the best rubber – but I picked up seventh in the second race. The meeting final was over as soon as it began. I went to put the car into gear when the green flag went down and the gearbox exploded. There was a dirty great hole in the side of the it, one of the teeth had come off and got stuck between the gears as they were turning. There was nowhere for them to go except outwards, ripping the casing to pieces as they did so. My race finished on the centre green without me even passing the green flag.

Back in the pits, Murray Harrison lent us a spare gearbox. The team worked efficiently to fit it and put our gearing in for the track which meant that I could get out in time for the Grand National, where I was flying to finish fourth. I came off slightly buoyed. Even though my tarmac gearbox had a massive hole in the side of it, I was happy with my pace on the track. If only I could catch those bloody cars in front.

The next day I ran in two heats, getting eighth and tenth. In the second race I had a new tyre on to try to get it ready for a meeting final, but I didn't get the best use out of it after I got into a bit of a pile-up with Gary Castell after a couple of laps. By the time I got going again I had Dave Riley right behind me. The car felt great, but I just couldn't get away from Dave. He stuck right behind me for a few laps as we circled through the traffic and I was trying to avoid being lapped by him. At the end I pulled off into the pits to find the guys with their heads in their hands.

'Tenth place?' they said. 'You did the wrong thing. You should have bought a new tarmac car instead of a new shale car, you couldn't even get away from a yellow top!'

'Hang on a second,' I replied. 'My car actually felt good there.' I knew what they were saying – it looked on track like I was being pushed around by a yellow top, but Dave was a very fast yellow top who was going really well. He won the race and was undergraded – the next time he raced he would be a red top.

A little miffed with the team, I went back out for the final, and again the car felt quick. I got legged up somewhere towards the start and I squabbled all race with Frankie, Mick and Tom. While we slowed each other down, the guys at the front shot away. Eventually, we four superstars came in sixth, seventh, eighth and ninth. Murray's gearbox had started to leak a bit of oil, so it was returned with our thanks and we loaded up before the Grand National.

The next week I checked the lap times on MyLaps. In the race where I felt I was quick but had Dave Riley pushing me, I actually got the second-fastest lap time of the whole meeting – and the fastest lap time belonged to Dave. I felt vindicated. The car was quick enough, it was just that we didn't have the best of luck throughout the meeting.

I was up against plenty. All the circumstances on track seemed to stack up in favour of the lower-graders. I wasn't at my freshest, having been on a stag do for one of my team, Mark Froggatt, on the Friday night. Couple that with a beer or two after the meeting on Saturday night (when we left the bar the bright dawn sun dazzled me, so it must have been a late finish!) and I perhaps didn't have the best preparation.

So not a bad weekend performance-wise, but not a great one for results. Still, the car was free from damage apart from the gearbox and the next meeting for it was the European Championship. I'd assured myself that I had some pace around Skegness, and the next race there would be the World Final. But before both of those, I had the chequered roof to defend.

A new car –
my cousin Michael and team members Michael and Ray
look on

12

There had been a lot of meetings so far that didn't really matter and maybe that was reflected in my performance. But the British Championship did matter. It mattered a lot. It was my title that I was defending, and I wanted to keep it. Had I not won the World Final then winning the British would have been the highlight of my career, so I was really keen to retain it.

Tom worked on my new shale car, getting it ready. I'd asked for certain things to be altered and I wanted the car to be bang on and ready to do battle from the first green flag. It wasn't ideal that my only two races to get used to the car would be the British Championship heats, but that's the way it goes!

Tom brought the car round to my bus in the pits at Coventry. There were still a few things left to do. I had to take the car to scrutineering and alter a few things in the cab to make sure I was comfortable. It was running a little warmer than I would have liked which gave me a bit of a concern. I'd had temperature issues in the Grand National that I won at Coventry, the last shale race I'd been in, but at the time I put that down to the muck screen coming loose. Now I had second thoughts – maybe there was something else at fault.

Bradley was sat in his car in the pit road, waiting to go out on track for the first of his heats in the Ministox British Championship, when I got a call saying that his engine sounded rough. I ran through the pits to find him and try to find out what the problem was – it sounded like the engine was being starved of fuel, probably there was muck in the carburettor or something. After a few minutes trying to get that sorted, the gate was closed without Bradley and he had to return to the back of the bus. I stripped his carburettor down and cleaned it out for him, all while the meeting officials were asking me to take part in a parade lap. There just wasn't time. Only when I was happy with his Mini could I concentrate on my stock car, and in no time the pit gate was closing.

I rolled out on track for perhaps the most uncomfortable race I've ever been in. The crutch strap came out of the seat where it was supposed to, but something wasn't right, and it was cutting me in half – in a place where you really don't want that to happen! Joking aside, Mark Taylor once crashed and his crutch strap injured him badly, he ended up with surgery on his important area. I was lined up on grid, a little worried to say the least, determined to keep out of trouble. The new car offered left-foot braking. My feet went down either side of the gearbox and there were two brake pedals, one on the left, one on the right. It was taking a bit of getting used to, even on the parade lap. I did a slow lap as the grid was getting ready, familiarising myself with the pedals. The first time I went to try to brake with my left foot, I missed and hit the clutch and went sliding towards the fence. Crikey, how was I going to overrule 25 years of experience of driving a stock car with right-foot braking? Throughout that first race, no matter how much I tried, as soon as I came into contact I reverted to autopilot and went back to right-foot braking. Still, I got a respectable fifth in my first race behind a gaggle of red tops. I was happy enough and still in one piece!

The temperature was still too high and I wasn't happy about it, but before the second heat all I had time to do was clean my goggles and sort out the seat straps. It was like sitting on a bed of feathers compared to the first race! Not that it helped me get a result, because as soon as the green flag dropped I realised that I had a flat outside rear tyre. It was most frustrating. You can't afford to have one bad result or you end up down the grid for the championship race. I knew that fifth in the first heat would be enough to qualify, but I wouldn't be at the front. As it turned out, I was on grid 18, the outside of the ninth row. There would be a lot of work to do to catch up with the likes of Tom, Mick, Frankie, Craig and track specialist Mark Gilbank towards the front.

With more of a gap between races, now we had a chance to work on the overheating engine. The fan was well away from the radiator and it had an effective cowling to suck the air directly into it, so we decided that it perhaps needed a fan spacer. Hopefully that would sort out the overheating.

I wasn't going to mess about. I was up for the race and wanted to get stuck in. I wasn't there to parade my chequered stripes for one last time and to make the numbers up, I wanted to try and make things happen. My plan was to get on the inside and get forward as rapidly as I could after the green flag dropped. Michael Scriven was on my inside, but behind him there was a gap where Adam Slater did not grid. In no time I pulled into the space and was on the inside line, making good progress. The yellows came out and I looked around to find that I was in sixth place. Murray Harrison and Frankie were in front. Looking down, the news was less good. The temperature gauge was rising, and to try and make progress in a race while you're coaxing the engine is not ideal.

I was in two minds: should I pull off while the yellows were out or keep going and rest the engine as much as possible? I decided to stay out on track and switch the engine off. A few minutes later they had cleared whatever obstruction brought out the yellows and I restarted the engine, but it wasn't long enough to make much difference. I was soon up to fifth, but the temperature was going higher and higher – unhealthily high – so I had to pull onto the infield.

I was absolutely gutted. To have to pull off for something like that was immensely frustrating. If I had carried on, everything would have continued getting hotter. The pistons and rings would have expanded and started to wear in the bores. The oil would have got hotter and thinner, not feeding the crankshaft bearings and camshaft bearings properly. Inevitably, something would have failed, leading to severe engine damage. It was a no-brainer to pull off. I was still tempted to carry on, though. If I had been up in the top two, in the place of Frankie or Murray, the decision would have been much harder. If I'd had a good engine, I could have been in the mix right at the end – Craig Finnikin took the race after starting the last lap in fourth – but ifs, buts and maybes don't count for anything after the chequered flag has waved.

As frustrating as anything else was the fact that I had an overheating engine and I didn't know why. The next meeting for this car would be the World Semi-Final at King's Lynn and I had a real problem to sort out. I had to find how to make the engine run cooler. We puzzled over it in the garage, trying to switch the radiator for a different one, removing mesh screens from around it, even boxing it in to try and stop shale getting through.

Was it a mistake to switch to the new Dave Riley car? I don't think so, because the problem was in the engine from the old car and it had already displayed signs that something wasn't right in the previous meeting.

What I was sure about was that I didn't want the major meetings to slip away from me while I was World Champion and then look back and think that I won bugger all with the gold roof. Last season, I won the British and then went from strength to strength to win my semi and then the World Final. This time I'd lost the British, but the semi and World Final were still to come.

Racing the defending champion in the European
Championship

13

It was an early start to get to Northampton for the next big meeting, the European Championship weekend. I wanted to get there early because there's nothing more frustrating than being in the area outside the main pits where you don't feel part of the meeting, away from most of the other drivers and the social scene. We parked up in a decent space and pulled the car from the bus. It was sporting a new gearbox because the old one which exploded at Skegness was damaged beyond economical repair. It had served me well for ten years, so I couldn't complain too much.

When I started the engine to take the car to scrutineering, the carburettor seemed to be flooding with fuel. We quickly stripped it down and found a bit of gunk in it, which was cleaned out and sorted the issue. Hopefully all the problems had been ironed out.

I didn't want to fall foul of the scrutineers a second time at the Euros. Last year I'd been caught out and it was all caused by good old British rain. When we pulled into the pits twelve months before, they were flooded. It was a right bloody mess. The track dried up for the Saturday night meeting, but on Sunday the weather couldn't make its mind up. Rain or sun? We weighed the car on the scales as usual expecting a dry race and there were no problems. Back at the bus, a bit of drizzle started, then it stopped. Then it drizzled again. And stopped again. The clouds looked ominous, so I made the call to swap both outside tyres for shale ones. As we were gridding up for the championship race, the rain started again. Happy that I'd made the right call, I had good grip during the race and managed to get second.

I hadn't considered the weight implications of changing the tyres. On being weighed after the race, my car was found to be four kilos too light. Tarmac tyres are heavier than shale tyres and the rims are two inches wider. So lacking two inches worth of wheel rim on two wheels and with lighter tyres, my car was the wrong side of the line. The officials made the right call in disqualifying me, but it was frustrating nonetheless. I can honestly say that it was the first championship race that I'm glad I didn't win – it would have been far more painful to have a title taken off me than a second place!

To set my mind at rest, the car was double-checked on the scales this time. There was a full meeting on Saturday evening, a chance to get everything sorted for the championship race, which was first up on Sunday. Looking to set a good marker for the weekend, I went out in the first heat. The marker was a pretty bad one, though. A half shaft broke, the first time I'd had a half shaft go since switching to a Transit back axle. It was a little frustrating and the timing could have been better, but nonetheless it wasn't too much of a crisis. There was no damage apart from the half shaft and there was still plenty of time to get it fixed and sort the car setup again. Sometimes you can have issues with getting a bust half shaft out and end up pulling the differential to pieces, but it came out just fine.

It was a little bit of a rush getting out for the consolation, but luckily everything seemed to be working out and I had a steady race, making sure that I qualified for the final in fifth place. It felt like I was travelling quite fast, but the lads back at the bus were moaning that I didn't seem to be cornering properly. I'd not given it much thought. I knew that the car wasn't handling fantastically, but I just put it down to the brakes. 'No,' they said, 'the pads were changed at Buxton and it doesn't seem to have done anything to improve the cornering.'

I went out for the final and focused on how the car went into the corners. They were right, it didn't seem to pull in enough. It didn't stop me having a decent race and finishing sixth, but towards the end of the race I could see that the outside front wheel was sparking. Something was catching, steel on steel, and when I got back to the pits we realised that the wheel bearing had collapsed. That must be it. We couldn't tell how long it had been wearing for, so we put the iffy brakes down to that. When the wheel bearing collapses you are in the lap of the gods, anything can happen, you can lose the whole inside of the wheel, but that didn't happen. Instead we just had to repair some damage on the hub and a bent stub axle, although it did mean missing the Grand National. Still, at least we'd solved the problem just in time for the championship race the following morning.

Or so I thought. Naively thinking that everything was fine, we all enjoyed a few pints in the bar and had a good party with the Dutch in Willie Peeters's tents. As always, the travelling Dutch created a good atmosphere – they had a DJ and we did a bit of singing, dancing, arm-wrestling and the general shenanigans I tend to get up to in Peter Falding's company.

The next day, I woke up ready for a good performance. The car was carrying the World Final setup which had proved itself ten months before. I started from the front of the superstars and hoped to repeat what I'd done at the World Final, get away from the chasing pack and splatter anybody who got in the way. I got a good green flag and stayed ahead of the rest, getting through a few of the slower reds and blues in front.

The car was quick, but the bloody brakes still weren't right. I couldn't throw the car through the corners as well as I wanted to, certainly not anywhere near as good as the World Final. When I found myself in a bit of track space and under no pressure, I started messing with the levers inside the cab, trying to alter something, but no matter what I tried I could not lock up the inside front wheel. Locking the inside front grabs the track, pulling the car to the inside, then you can back it up a little bit so it doesn't smoke. It means that the car holds a good line through the corner but doesn't wreck the tyres, and it's something that I'm usually pretty good at. Now, however, I couldn't get the wheel to lock and my speed and line through the corner were suffering.

Mick Sworder caught up, desperate to retain his title, and we traded blows over a series of corners. Gary Castell was pulled into the mix, but then Scott Davids saw his chance and planted Mick and I onto Gary. Having rejoined a lap down, I decided that to carry on racing was futile. My car wasn't 100% and some of the superstars had got well ahead. I was wearing my tyres for nothing. I retired to the infield.

Back in the pits, I parked up and moaned. The team had a look about and decided to change the pads on the inside front wheel, this time putting on a tougher compound. Back on track for the heat, it didn't make the slightest difference. I finished in ninth so qualified for the final, but the car did not feel right. The lads were still moaning, saying 'there's something you're not doing right.'

I replied, 'it isn't me, I know how to drive a bloody stock car! It's an issue with the car!' I was steaming mad and retreated to the bus, not even stopping to take my helmet off, and sat there for five minutes just to calm down. It didn't completely work and I said to the lads, 'just load up, I'm sick of it, we're wasting our time. You think it's me, I think it's the car, just stick it in the back of the bus.'

The team and I don't fall out very often. I'll usually come off after a race and I can see in their faces everything that I need to know. They might offer some advice – you should have done this, you shouldn't have done that – but more often than not I'm already thinking the same thing and I'll be in full agreement. I already know why they are disgruntled. One sarcastic comment is often enough to get their point across. Generally, there is great banter in the team – even when I'm crap!

But on this occasion, I couldn't put my finger on what was wrong. I could see that they weren't happy. Michael, who is a little younger and less experienced than the other members of the team, was bubbling over with frustration. The others – Raymond, Brian and even the unflappable Lee – were a little more belligerent than usual and getting pissed off. But I was pissed off too.

Michael and Lee got chatting in the pits to another team and someone suggested that we check the reducing valve to the nearside front brake. It set us thinking. The valve is there so you can alter the force to the brake and make sure it doesn't lock up. It might be that failing, stopping enough pressure getting to the brake and causing a problem. With nothing to lose, we decided that we would try changing it, although in 25 years of racing I'd never had an issue with one. At some point we would need to identify the problem before the World Final and this would be another thing ticked off the list, but I wasn't confident that it would solve the problem.

With a new valve on, I was sent up the pits to try it out. I pressed the brake pedal and immediately the wheel locked. For crying out loud! Something as simple as that, after we'd tried everything else!

Relations in the team were restored. There was no need for anybody to apologise, we just got on with it and came back together as a team. Raymond and Brian are the old hands who have seen it all before, both with me and my dad, and it was like water off a duck's back to them. Lee is very laid back – so much so that he's almost horizontal, he doesn't do getting stressed. And Michael was happy too – he just wants to see me do better, he knows what I'm capable of; to see me languishing in the lower places frustrates him.

With better brakes, I went out for the final. I went round the track while we lined up and tested the brakes.

The wheel locked up again. Bearing in mind that the car functioned well on Saturday apart from the brakes, I now felt confident. When the green flag fell, I took the first corner like I was on rails. The car pulled up perfectly and I got past some of the red tops by the end of the first lap. The yellow flags were waved almost immediately and I counted up the cars in front – I was already in tenth. The green flag fell again and I took the next corner well, getting nice and close to Ed Neachell. Then the clutch exploded.

Think of as many swear words as you can. I shouted all those and more as I pulled off. This meeting had proved to be yet another tale of woe. Paul Hines went on to win the final. I had already passed him and I knew that my car was quick, I just had gremlins that I couldn't shake off.

I was having more reliability issues than I'd ever had and I was spending more time in the garage than ever before. I now had damage to the clutch on the back of the previous tarmac meeting when the gearbox went. The clutch again was the problem the meeting before that.

It was nice for Tom Harris to win the European Championship. He was quite emotional and overcome by it all. He has been so close to success in the past, knocking on the door for some time, but he just couldn't quite get over the finish line first. There is a feeling of disbelief when you finally win something you've aimed for – and I should know – so I was very pleased for Tom, and Mick, Sharon and Jamie too. We were parked just to the side of them and could play a little role in the celebrations.

There is no jealousy when I see people like Tom and Craig win the European and British titles. I've won those championships before and I realise that although I try to win every championship I can, there are other drivers trying to do the same. However, I admit that I used to find it very painful watching other drivers win the World Final. I'd look at them on the top step – whether it was an established name like John Lund winning his eighth or Andy Smith winning his fifth, or somebody like Murray Harrison or Keith Chambers coming from further back to win – and I'd think 'you'd better be appreciating this, because I know how much it would mean to me if I won.' The thought that they might take being World Champion for granted used to cripple me.

Now that I'd won the World Championship, I thought I could help somebody celebrate it. But they would have to take it off me first.

A few words of fatherly advice –
probably 'pull your bloody finger out!'

14

Everybody has talked for years about the curse of the gold roof, where World Champions have a rubbish season after winning the World Final. It certainly struck my dad, who didn't win a meeting final in all the time he was World Champion. As soon as he lost the title in 1983 to Stuart Smith, he promptly won the meeting final – so at least he won one final under the gold roof, even if he officially shouldn't have been using it! Previously I thought that the curse is a load of tosh, but looking back at my season so far, I realised that it looked pretty tame. Rubbish, really. I'd had nothing but bad luck and disastrous results. Was this how I wanted to be remembered?

I had started to question everything. Was it my commitment that wasn't right? Was it my car setup? Was my ability starting to fail me?

However, every cloud had a silver lining. I knew that I would be totally written out of everybody's mind when it came to my chances of retaining the gold roof. Spectators would be looking at the drivers around me on the semi-final grid – Craig Finnikin in front, Stuart Smith Junior behind, Dan Johnson to my side, Frankie Wainman Junior on pole. Even those drivers would not be considering me a challenger. Nobody would consider little old Paul Harrison. Maybe that could be a good thing – I could fly under the radar to the World Final.

I wouldn't say that I was confident – I couldn't be after the bad luck I'd had over the past few weeks – but I was hopeful of a good finish. Starting from fourth place on the grid, in an ideal world I wanted to be first or second to start in front of the first row of foreigners in the World Final, but more realistically I would accept a top five finish.

The new shale car had been overheating at the British Championship so before we took it down to King's Lynn for the World Semi-Final we spent a few hours in the garage trying to get the temperature down. Now I just needed a nice, relaxing build up to the race. If only. Bradley went out in a Ministox heat before the semi-final and I watched him from near the pits. Towards the end of the race, the steering arm on the nearside hub snapped. It flicked his inside wheel onto right-hand lock just as he entered the turn and the Mini went full speed into the fence. You can picture how much the steering had gone because he hit the fence with his inside front corner. My first thought, as always, was to worry whether he was ok. The impact was hard and it would have been a difficult one to brace for. Once it was clear that he was fine, we could have a look at the car. It absolutely wrecked the corner of the body, smashing the body shell and damaging the wheel hub. The inside rear had been clipped by a car early on in the race and was bent as well. We were busy working on his car, trying to get it ready for the rest of the meeting, while I had marshals nagging in my ear saying that they needed me on the grid for the semi-final. Most of the other drivers were probably getting in the zone and concentrating on their own race, making last-minute adjustments to their cars. I had none of that; my stock car was parked up and totally ignored while we worked on the bloody Ministox! It's not ideal preparation to go into combat, running round after another car. The same thing happened at the British Championship, when Bradley's carburettor needed cleaning out. I'm not the only driver who has to deal with looking after other cars. Frankie Wainman Junior has spent much of the past few years working on Phoebe and Frankie JJ's Ministox and Danny's stock car when he could have been working on his own, and his results may have suffered as a result.

You can only cut yourself so finely and ultimately it stops you performing at your best.

Luckily, the car setup had already been altered with the right tyres and stagger for the King's Lynn track. The track looked perfect. It wasn't overwatered and there would be a good racing line within a couple of laps. The engine temperature after the rolling lap was reading quite well, so hopefully the garage time had dealt with the problem.

Sitting on the grid was a little surreal. I was in unknown territory. It didn't feel right, not like other semi-finals. Normally, the semi is a tense meeting. It's about keeping the dream alive. Every season the World Final is what it had all been about for me and the semi-final is a crucial link in the chain – it's a stepping stone that you need to cross, but the fear is that you'll trip up and fall in. Realistically, you know that you need to be in the top five to stand a chance in the World Final, although if an incident happens and you drop down the order, then the panic is just about trying to qualify so you can be part of the big race. Even if you get through, you probably won't have a chance of winning. At some point, the dream would fail – either in the semi-final or the big race itself. There's an old saying that there's always next year, but it gets a little hard hearing that time after time. I would laugh it off, but nonetheless it's painful!

This year, the desperation that I would normally feel about needing to qualify, and qualify well, wasn't there. I can remember strapping myself in on the home straight.

Lee and Michael were on the track with me after the parade lap, but then the moment came when they said good luck and I was left to myself. At that point it is just you and the car. It's a lonely place, all the preparation boils down to this moment and the stress and tension are almost tangible, but this time it wasn't there. It didn't feel like a semi-final, it was just another race.

Whether having a clear head helped me at the start I don't know, but as far as I was concerned this race would be all about the green flag. I was vulnerable on the outside of the second row and wanted to quickly get into a safer place and not get caught in a first bend scuffle. As the cars started to enter the last turn on the rolling lap, I could see that the track surface looked good on the home straight. There should be plenty of drive there, so I wanted to get a good run down the track and slip into third place on the first turn.

Dan Johnson was on the inside, the driver who I would need to get in front of on the straight, but he got a good start and beat me away. Will Yarrow, behind him, was a little slower off the mark. There was a gap for me to glide into on the first bend. I'd got safe straight away, which wasn't guaranteed with Stuart Smith Junior starting behind me!

In a relatively comfortable position, I could take stock over the first couple of laps. The car was pushing on a little bit into corners. With all the faffing about with the tarmac car and sorting out the overheating problem in the shale car, I hadn't been able to iron out all the little niggles.

If I'm driving a car that I'm not 100% happy with on shale, you'll often see me pushing on in corners. If you try to take a corner at full belt and whip the steering wheel round, you can overcook it and either go skidding out wide towards the fence and let a load of cars through or you can even spin and put yourself out of contention. Instead, I'll tend to be cautious. Better off to push on a little bit, braking and turning slightly later with a little bit of understeer, knowing that you are still in full control of the car and at some stage the front end will grip and drive the car round the corner. Fancy driving, sliding about and swinging the back end out, can come later.

The push meant that Stuart and Will got in front on the second lap, but it only took a lap to get back past Will and in front of Dan. Frankie and Craig were up front exchanging positions; I was racing for third place with Stuart. He got away from me, then I passed him and he sat behind for a while until he came back at me and I dropped to fourth.

Shortly after a restart, about halfway through the race, the first three broke away a little bit and Dan came past after running us both wide into the fence. Then Paul Hines worked his way through and I was in sixth, below what I considered to be the minimum acceptable result. The yellow flags waved again with four laps to go as the race was starting to drift away from me. But then a bit of luck.

I gained a place during the stoppage when Dan pulled off because he was overheating. It was bad luck for him, but at least I was back in the top five. I was well aware that the same problem had been plaguing me, so I had an eye on my own temperature gauge. It was rising again, although not as hot as at the British Championship. More importantly, the radiator wasn't kicking out water so it was maintaining some cooling ability. As long as it did, I was happy to keep going.

Then, on the restart, I took an inside line through the first turn, down the back straight and into the last turn and managed to get in front of Paul. Now, with just three laps to go, a little bit of track space and a slicked up surface, I tried flicking the back end out. It felt all right, I still had full control, and with a slightly faster line I started to gain a little ground on the cars in front.

The car felt nice and loose as we went into the last lap. Had there been a couple more laps I felt I could have been starting to push for the front, but as it was Frankie had a good lead, Stuart was second, Craig was third and I was fourth. Going into the turn at the end of the home straight, Stuart overcommitted and took himself out wide. Craig went up the inside and I closed right in on Stuart as we went down the back straight. He was still a little out of sorts and I managed to get on him. I got my front bumper just inside Stuart's back bumper, and as Stuart got back on the racing line we snagged up slightly. Stuart's back end twisted towards the fence and his front end towards the infield. I kept the pressure on because I didn't feel threatened. Stuart would have tried to shake me off towards the infield and as he did so it put him tight towards the tyres. I drifted off and kept a good line into the bend, but Stuart was too close to the inside and from that position he was going to naturally drift a little wider than he would like. I only had to bob his back inside bumper to make him go wider, then I ran into the back corner of his nerf rail which kept him out wide for longer with his front end pointing towards the fence. None of them were big hits, just enough to disrupt his natural line. By the time we hit the home straight, I was up his inside and away for third.

Even if Stuart hadn't got a little bit snagged, I would have been there to have a lunge. I wouldn't have gone for a suicide dive, but I was always in position for a good measured hit to ensure that I would have gained a place. There are some drivers who say that they would sit in place if it suited them and settle for a lower position, but I have never done that in a World Championship Semi-Final. If I haven't won a semi, it isn't because I have settled for second, third, fourth or whatever. The position I get is always the best I can achieve on that day, in that race.

In truth, the race had not been all that exciting; nobody landed any big hits which can sometimes happen in a semi-final. But I had to be happy with third. I would have preferred to have been in front of the foreigners – the difference between finishing second and third is to start on either row 2 or row 4 – but at one point I was fighting for fifth or sixth. Had I finished in that position, I would have been totally bagged off. As defending World Champion, I shouldn't be fighting for fifth or sixth in the semi. I felt I could hold my head high.

So I knew I'd be on the fourth row of the World Final, but who else would be around me? Frankie, Craig and Stuart were also there, but the second semi-final at Birmingham would decide the rest of the grid. I could enjoy a relatively low-key meeting with all the attention on the other semi.

Changing the clutch on the tarmac car for the second time in a matter of weeks proved to be a bit of a problem. I have a plastic clutch aligning tool which we use to set the clutch up. It is always a bit awkward, but this time it was a nightmare. Instead of taking ten or fifteen minutes to get in place, this time the hours dragged on. No matter how much shuffling around we tried, it wouldn't go in place. I was starting to get really annoyed, wondering if we were even going to make it to Birmingham that weekend.

'Stuff it,' I announced to the rest of the lads, 'let's not bother going.'

'Don't you want to watch the semi-final?' Ray asked.

At that moment, I really wasn't arsed. Lee, ever the calm presence, told me to see how I felt in the morning. Anguish in the garage is not my favourite feeling, and he could tell I was frustrated. The next day, I went across to see Peter Falding and borrow a metal clutch aligning tool of his. It was the fact that the clutch was beating me that was annoying me, more than the thought of missing the semi-final. I'd done it many times before and I wasn't going to let it get the better of me. I took an extended lunch break, wandered down to the garage with Peter's tool and ragged the clutch about until I got it in. Success! I fired off a celebratory text to the lads telling them that I'd sorted it and that we'd be going at the weekend, and they came down to the garage the following evening to get the car weighed and loaded up. They were probably relieved that I was in a better mood as much as that they were going to see the racing!

It was supposed to be a simple meeting with all the pressure on the boys in the semi-final. Paul Hines parked up next to me in the pit lane before our heat and commented that we should have an easy drive to the final since so many of the top guys were waiting for the semi. Always one to liven up a dull race, on the first lap Rob Cowley chose to drive up the bank and Ed Neachell finished on his roof. So much for a nice, steady race! Time for a complete restart.

Knowing that it should be a low-pressure race, I went out with an old tyre on the inside rear wheel. It made the handling far too loose, the tyre was slowly failing, but even so I was on course for a top three or four finish. I struggled on and was going past the starter – rattle, rattle, bang – when all this blooming noise signalled that something was wrong. Again! For crying out loud, how many more demons could I be struck by? I parked up by the fence, demoralised again. I could tell it was the clutch, gearbox or differential, something in the drive line, not the engine.

A quick investigation turning the wheels in the pits showed that the prop shaft was not turning, so it was the differential that had gone. It was the first differential problem we'd had since transferring to a Transit back axle eighteen months before. Transit diffs have a reputation of being a little bit temperamental, they have to be set right or they can cause a host of problems and we don't really know much about the goings on in there other than to take the back plate off and check the whip. It could have proved the end of the meeting, but Lee is a trained Ford mechanic and has had some dealings with Transits in the past, so he decided to have a look and see what he could make of it. The pinion had sheared all the teeth off the crown wheel. 'We can do this if we can find somebody who has got the bits,' Lee announced.

Glen set about getting all the bits of crap out of the casing and Will Yarrow came to have a nose around. He had a differential with the correct gearing in for us, one that he doesn't use, so we quickly agreed to take it off his hands and buy him one back that was suitable for his own setup. We scrounged the other bits we needed. The semi-final got in the way of our repairs so we didn't make it in time for the consolation and final, but we were able to get back on track in time for the Grand National. Murray stuck his head under the back of the car as we made the final adjustments and declared that everything looked fine. I put a decent tyre on the inside rear instead of the scrapper that I'd run in the heat because I wanted to get an accurate reflection of how the car was running. The next time it would be used was the first tarmac round of the Shootout, back here at Birmingham.

I fought to get out of the traffic when the green flags fell, but before I knew what was happening I was facing the wrong way, hooked up with Lee Fairhurst near the fence. The race was as good as over in terms of getting a decent finish and normally I would have pulled off, but I needed to give the car a proper blast. Mark Gilbank, who had won the final, was just behind me and pushing to get past as I pulled out from the tangle with Lee. I knew that he was travelling quickly, but then I started to pull away from him. Once I was in some clear space, it felt fantastic. The speed down the straights was good and it was pulling up nicely through the corners. Nobody would have noticed me, I was well out of the race nearly a lap down, but I was much happier. The lads were nodding their heads afterwards, they said I looked quick from their perspective too. MyLaps provided the final confirmation, I was nearly two-tenths of a second faster than the rest of the grid. I knew I had the speed, I was just missing the reliability and luck.

The end of the meeting offered a chance to summarise where we were at and what was coming up. The other semi-final had been a good race. Everybody was totally committed. I thought Mat Newson might chicken out of the first bend and let Mick Sworder through, but he didn't. All the drivers went into the first lap like they wanted to win the race. Tom Harris got squeezed out and went down to sixth or seventh, but rather than going crazy and trying to get back immediately he bided his time and waited until he had a bit of room around him. He got his chance when somebody dropped some oil. Lee Fairhurst was most unfortunate – he was away and looked good for the win but was first to the oil and went in the fence. Lee told me afterwards that his fuel tap was loose and swinging. When he impacted with the fence, the tap swung into the off position and cut his fuel supply. On the rolling lap after the restart, once his fuel line was exhausted, the engine just died. I felt for him. It's not very often that a tarmac specialist will be lucky enough to get a tarmac semi-final and World Final, and Lee's dream appeared to be dead in the water. Mat Newson was unlucky too – he climbed up the wall behind Lee and was out of the semi-final for the second year in a row. That left Tom and Mick to have a tactical race to the finish. I think that they would both have been happy with second. Both their lap times dropped by over a second as each was politely saying to the other 'please, after you', until Tom looked in his mirror and saw Danny Wainman coming. He wasn't of that train of thought! They had to speed up and race to the finish.

I was back in the pits while the coin toss went on for pole position at Skegness, so it was a little later that I heard that Frankie Wainman Junior was on pole with Mick Sworder next to him. The coin toss also meant that the rest of the grid shuffled into place. Tom Harris and Craig Finnikin made up the second row, two foreign drivers would be seeded onto the third row. Because Frankie won the coin toss, I was on the inside of the fourth row next to Danny Wainman. Ryan Harrison and Stuart Smith Junior were on the fifth row, with two more foreigners behind them.

That wouldn't be a bad place to start. Maybe it was a good thing I didn't get one place higher in the semifinal, because Frankie winning the coin toss would have put me on the outside of the second row. I'd managed to get through that safely enough at King's Lynn, but didn't want to be there at Skegness. With Ryan behind me, Stuart just across and Rob Speak lurking on row 7, there would be every chance of a big push going into the first corner. The inside of the fourth row was likely to be that little bit safer.

It would make a pleasant change, anyway. I had been on the outside of the last four World Finals, and sometimes that can be your undoing. I was on the outside of the second row at Coventry in 2010 and I didn't make it past the first corner.

I was confident, but confidence doesn't win races. I'd been confident in plenty of other races so far this year and somebody had pissed on my chips. It was time to forget about everybody else and concentrate on my own preparation for my biggest race with the gold roof.

Waiting for the green flag at Coventry

15

The Birmingham semi-final meeting was the last one at that track before the first round of the Shootout. The next meeting, at Coventry, would be my last one there before the second round of the Shootout. I really needed to be getting both cars sorted for the most vital part of the season.

In the newsletter before the meeting, we were given notice that the powers-that-be had decided to alter the restart protocol. In future, under yellow flag situations, rather than restart in single file in the system which has been used for years, they were going to form up a new grid. The driver leading the race would choose the outside or inside line and everybody else would shuttle into place.

The impact of the change was obvious. It would make each restart a much bigger spectacle. Twice the amount of cars in the same space is going to lead to more bumper work, better for the spectators, better for the promoters because the fans are happy, but it would create more damage and more hassle for the drivers. The same letter indicated that the powers were aware that there were issues with car numbers and the expense of competing. It was a complete contradiction. You can't try to bring down the cost of the sport at the same time as introducing a new system that would inevitably cause more damage. Get real.

You can imagine what would happen in the situation if this method was used during a World Final. Every restart would be like the first bend of a race. That's the last thing you want as a driver. It's painful enough to have gained an advantage and be leading the race by good fortune or good driving only to have it taken away by a caution, never mind the added stress and danger caused by a reformed grid. Had this rule been used in the 2011 World Final, rather than restarting twice behind Frankie I would have been on the outside of the front row. The driver on the inside of the second row would have shut the door on me into the first corner. There's no way I would have won the race from that position.

There was a pre-meeting drivers briefing and during that it was evident that none of the drivers were happy. Ultimately, the officials were forced to yield. They said that they understood our concerns and would put the new method under review. It had been raining before the meeting so it wouldn't have been the best conditions to try out something new anyway, but that turned into a convenient excuse to put it aside. Although I had feelings on the issue, I didn't need to say much. The younger bucks had plenty to say on my behalf, instead I stood with John Lund chuckling at the drivers who got hot under the collar.

Getting used to the new shale car was still an ongoing process. The brakes were a little iffy in the heat so I was unable to get through the field as far as I'd like and finished in twelfth. Usually it's the first twelve that qualify at Coventry and we settled down to tinker with the brakes and make the adjustments required. Then one of the marshals came up to me and said, 'aren't you going out for the consolation?' It turned out that only the first ten qualified from the heats, so I jumped in and raced out on track. The comments from the team – 'just make it to the final this time, will you?' – helped motivate me to second place. It was surprisingly hectic – one or two drivers were getting under my feet and slowing me up and the conditions seemed to exaggerate the dodgy brakes. I wasn't aware that I was in second place behind Danny Wainman, otherwise I'd have pushed harder for the win!

We'd put a bigger radiator in the car in an attempt to eradicate the overheating issue once and for all. In the first race, running from cold, the car ran a lot cooler than it had done before. It also ran cooler during the rest of the meeting, still not quite as cool as I would like, but significantly better. It was maintaining the water level too, which was a good sign.

The run out in the consolation gave me another chance to think about the brake settings and adjust them slightly, and I put on a new outside rear tyre for the final. I was pole superstar, which although sounds good, meant that I was the worst superstar on shale. Still, the little bit of clear track in front meant that I was off like a rocket down the home straight when the green flags were waved. I took a decent line through the corner, but then Mat Newson came out of nowhere, straight across the corner, running up my inside front wheel and getting stuck. Although I managed to rejoin, I had no brakes at all. Mat had sheared my brake pipe. I'd not even completed one lap and I was on the infield.

We had both beaten John Lund away from the start and Mat should have been more careful on the first turn. It wasn't a vindictive move – he won't need a punishment tap – it was over-exuberance. He just screwed up and took us both out of the race. He was a sloppy git, and I told him so on the way to the bar after the meeting.

'You're experienced now, you shouldn't be making errors like that on the first corner!'

'You should have got going quicker!' Mat answered. Nonetheless, I thought he drove like a cock.

There wasn't much point in using the brand new tyre for the Grand National, so we saved that for another day and put a worn tyre on. Again, it was a hectic race, as races often are at Coventry with thirty cars on an overwatered track. Cars were spinning off in all directions but I had a couple of breaks and by the end of the race was up to fourth. We'd got the brakes sorted and for a change it felt like they were doing what I wanted them to. Once or twice I should have committed a little more but I held back and it caused me to push on, but in the main the car felt good. I was as fast as anybody else on track and Frankie was the only driver to pass me – he started the car behind me and finished a car or two in front with a couple of lower graders. I'd suffered no damage other than the brake pipe and nearside front bumper stay that Mat had damaged.

Next up was supposed to be a meeting at Stoke, but there was a change of plan. Lindsey does not have much to say on when or where I race, leaving me to play with my toys pretty much unhindered, but leading up to the Stoke meeting I was having such a run of bad luck that she stepped in. We were due to fly out to Ibiza the day after. The plan was that I would race at Stoke, drive to a hotel at East Midlands airport, get showered and maybe grab a couple of hours sleep, then go on holiday.

Lindsey said, 'don't you think it would be better to miss Stoke? Then we can have a steady drive down on Saturday and relax a little bit to start the holiday.' No doubt she also realised the mood I'd be in if I had yet another crap meeting! Instead of racing I enjoyed a far more relaxing swim, sauna and Jacuzzi, followed up by a nice meal and drink while watching Mo Farah win gold in the Olympics. It was a great idea from Lindsey and started the holiday in a completely different light.

The holiday also meant that we missed the Gold Cup meeting at Venray. My sister was in Holland to see it; she had gone across with her boyfriend, Daniel Harter, along with Lisa and Andy Smith, who wanted to check on the car he had built for Geert Jan Keijzer. Vicky texted to tell me that Tom Harris had won the title, following up the European Championship with another great victory. I sent Tom a text of congratulation, saying something along the lines of, 'nice one, I've heard that you won. The next pint I'll have will be for you, from my lounger by the pool in the belting sun!'

I ticked that box many years ago. I used to go across to Baarlo and had the spectacle of racing on the long track there. Once a year for three or four years on the trot we crossed the channel as part of the exodus to Europe. It was great to do something completely different, and it was a social occasion as much as a driving one. It was the time when Peter Falding and John Lund were both doing really well on the long track, and the Tyldesleys and Maynards would usually be there as well. My team would travel down in the early hours of Friday morning, usually after going to a nightclub on Thursday evening to get us all in the mood. We would continue the party on the ferry across and by Friday evening we'd be enjoying a few drinks in Holland. After a day and night of leisure on Saturday, the business of racing would finally begin at Baarlo on Sunday, followed by a dash home to be back at work on Monday.

The first year I went to Baarlo, 1990, was probably the most tiring. I took across a new coach that I shared with Warren Hunter, the maiden voyage for the transporter bus. After a heavy weekend of drinking and racing, we charged back across the channel, only pausing for a well-needed breakfast at a Little Chef. From there, we drove straight back to the yard and switched to the shale car, then drove across to Scunthorpe for another race meeting. I was absolutely shattered, but the adrenaline must have been kicking in because I went out on track and had one of my best ever meetings – wins in the heat and final and third in the Grand National. The things you can get away with when you're young!

Things have changed now. The racing takes place all day on Saturday and Sunday, and the trip across is much more a racing weekend rather than a social weekend. The Dutch cars have different regulations to do with the brakes and a few other bits, so as well as a busy weekend racing, it would mean a busy build up in the garage in the week before to make the modifications required. Rather than being a holiday, racing at the Gold Cup would be a serious venture. Would I like to go again? Never say never, but I think that I've been there and done that.

The fixture organisers are partly to blame too. I think that it's important to have some family time during the season and with the kids being in school we only have the six-week summer holiday to get a decent break together. All the important race meetings seem to be crammed into that period. Looking ahead to next year, it looks like there will be a semi-final in the last weekend of July, just after the kids break up from school. Then, a fortnight later, there is the other semi-final. Immediately after that is the Gold Cup at Venray, and no doubt after that the Shootout will start. Something has to give, and while I'm committed to the World Championship and Shootout, it's the Gold Cup that will have to go.

Pedal to the metal!

16

The Gold Cup might have been skipped, but the gold roof race was on the horizon. And before that, the race for silver began. The cut-off point for the top twelve point scorers had passed and I was comfortably among them, despite a poor season. Once the attendance points had been added, I went into the series in ninth place out of twelve. I was keen to make an impression and jump up the table as soon as possible.

I was well prepared. The previous meetings that each car had raced were at Birmingham and Coventry, where the first two Shootout rounds would be held. Moreover,

I'd left both thinking that the cars were running pretty well.

There's more to preparation that just setting up the car, though. I should have been out to practice at Birmingham, at least to warm the tyres and brakes up, but I didn't. Maybe I was a bit lazy. Instead I started the first heat at Birmingham a little gingerly, easing the car into the meeting. A couple of laps in, the yellow flags were waved. I was behind Dan Johnson on the restart, but it was clear that his car was struggling. I sat right up his backside, waiting for him to pull off on the rolling lap, but he stayed on the racing line. As we exited the final turn onto the home straight, it was obvious he wasn't going anywhere. Just as I realised that I needed to get round the outside, the drivers behind me thought the same thing and Mike James ran into my outside rear tyre with his front bumper as we scrambled to the outside of the track. It put a big hole in the tyre and immediately the car sagged to one side. First race of the Shootout and already I was out of it.

I was a bit frustrated with Dan. It was evident that he'd got a problem, perhaps he was trying to correct whatever had gone wrong with his car, but he only lasted another half-lap before he pulled onto the centre green. We were all blaming Dan back in the pits, but all we could do was change the tyre and get out for the next heat. Typically for the Shootout, all the lads at the back were charging into each other. After a handful of laps, I went into a corner attacking with my front bumper while being attacked from the rear at the same time. Suddenly everything died. Something had gone wrong with the electrics; the ignition went and the engine stalled. Another DNF. I knew that I would be able to race in the final because of low car numbers at the meeting, but I'd only be racing for half points because I had not qualified from the heats. On the infield, I lifted up the bonnet and could see that the negative coil wire had come off. I reattached it and the engine fired up with no problem so I could drive back to the pits. It was just one of those things. I clamped all the wires back on more securely, changed the tyre and made my way back out on grid for the final.

As much as anything, I was racing just to make sure that some of the other guys finished one place further back to deny them a few points. Still, it was a good race. We exchanged a few hard blows, front and back. Tom Harris managed to get away and get a bit of a gap while I got involved in a race with Dan. I should have given him a harder hit at some stage than I did. Although I was giving him reasonable taps, I was trying to shake off Lee Fairhurst from behind and I was also aware that all the other Shootout drivers were behind him. If I got involved with a big hit on Dan, it could take me wide and then they would be right up with us, so I settled in behind him to pull a gap on the cars behind. Then Dan made a couple of good manoeuvres and got away from me, sneaking past Shaun Blakemore. I finished just behind in fourth. Back in the pits, Tom was having a few problems with his car on the scales. It was on and off as he struggled to make the car fit the weight ratios it needed to. I realised that if I'd hit Dan harder and got past, it might have been me finishing in second. Then, if Tom failed scrutineering, maybe I would pick up a win.

Back on track for the Grand National, there was a little delay. Tom eventually came out and took a position at the front, evidently he hadn't infringed any regulations and made his car legal. By this time it was drizzling, but fortunately we had just changed the inside rear tyre for a slightly softer compound because we expected a damp track. Dan started in front of me – I seemed to spend the entire meeting looking at his back bumper – and he got away well. My car felt very good and driveable, although I had an outside front tyre which was past its best and caused a bit of a push. I kept with Dan, locked up slightly on the exit of a turn and Frankie came past, three abreast down the straight. Lee Fairhurst took that opportunity to fire Scott Davids across my bows, which rattled me and I gave the fence a good bite. I shook off Scott after bouncing out of the fence and quickly checked round – no damage. My tyres had come up to temperature and I could tell that I was catching Lee, who had pulled a gap after he came past. I got a good shot on Lee and took his place off him on the last bend to finish sixth. I was pleased with that. The move on Lee was warranted because he was the one who had delayed me with Scott Davids. It's all about points at Shootout meetings. Normally you just go for the win and it makes little difference if you finish second or seventh. During the Shootout, every place and every point is significant. Who knows what that last bender on Lee might mean at the end of the series?

I had salvaged something from the meeting, seventeen points after a poor start, and I was still in the game. In fact, I'd moved up to sixth.

Off we went to round two, at Coventry the following weekend. When we got there, we were told to park miles away in the rear pits by the pit marshal. We were well away from the atmosphere of the meeting. They wanted to maintain the main pit space for Formula 1s only, so Formula 1 drivers with a Ministox in tow were put out with the rest of the Minis round the back. I wasn't happy and I remonstrated with the promoter. Surely the punters who were coming through the gate wanted to see the Shootout drivers, never mind the gold top car, and Frankie Wainman Junior and I were missing from the main pits. A few spectators came to see me after the heats and told me that they didn't even realise I was there until they saw me on track – they'd been looking out on their pit walk but hadn't brought binoculars so hadn't spotted me. I thought that the Shootout drivers should have had their own section, and Bradley and little Frankie could have easily parked their Minis to one side.

It might seem like nothing, but being in the pits and chatting to spectators is one of the things that I enjoy. Spectators like to chat to the drivers too, or just observe them at work. Anyway, the real result is that I got a little riled up. Maybe that would help my racing!

The car numbers were high enough that we'd have a heat and consolation format so if I didn't qualify for the final this time I wouldn't be out there on track. The Shoot-out drivers were split through the heats and I had been put with Frankie and Craig as the main opposition. We had a good race. I had set the brakes weighted a little more towards the rear so I was able to chuck the car into the corners using the drive method, getting sideways much earlier. It's a style that I've never previously adopted. At the beginning of the race, I sometimes lose ground due to understeer. The idea behind the new setup was that the car would handle much better in the early laps, and I found, at least on this occasion, that it worked. Frankie, Craig and I worked our way towards the front. I got a good measured shot on Frankie at one point and got up his inside, but then spotted one of Mat Newson's hire cars with its nose sticking in the fence and the back out onto the track. I expected a yellow flag, but it didn't come. As I shut off a little early, waiting for the yellows, Frankie launched me into the fence. It was a fair old shot and he easily came up the inside. I spent a couple of laps seeing a few stars. I was still waiting for them to rescue the car, but they didn't and I never had the opportunity to recover my head. Craig and Frankie were the only ones to get past though, and I came in a decent third place.

I was travelling well in the final too, cutting through the pack after a couple of stoppages, when another yellow flag brought everybody back together. I was in a good position, right amongst it with just over half the race gone. The greens fell and I was just making ground on the front-runners when I finished up in a little bit of a ruck which forced me round the outside of a couple of cars that were tangled. I almost became part of it myself, and having just passed a load of cars over a few laps, they all got back in front of me again. By this time Craig was off into the sunset – he had a good run and made his own luck and well deserved his third Coventry final win in succession. I got my head down for the last few laps and was fortunate that a few other drivers got in a bit of a mess, so I ended up finishing seventh. At one point, I had been looking for a much better finish than that.

Part of the schedule was the Fathers Race in the Ministox, but I chose not to take part. It was a full weekend of racing for the Minis and the Fathers Race was on Saturday night. I didn't want to go out on track and risk the car – we don't carry loads of spares so if I damaged Bradley's car it would be the end of his weekend. As his Ministox career comes to an end, I didn't want him to miss out. That said, I might as well have raced and destroyed it for how well he did on the Sunday. He was bloody useless!

Back in the day when my dad was a regular driver at Long Eaton, we saw Ministox for the first time. The formula had been started by Keith Barber a season or two before, and at some point my dad got chatting to him. Dad asked, 'would our Paul be able to have a go?' Keith apparently answered, 'can he drive?' My dad said, 'of course he can, I taught him!'

So, although the age limits for Ministox ran from ten to just before sixteen, I turned out on track for my first race in 1977 when I was eight. My reward for gaining my 25-metre swimming badge was to have the Mini signwritten and it had Willie Harrison Junior plastered over it. I eventually earned plenty of race wins and my best championship results came in my last year, when I got second in both the British Championship and National Championship. Second in major championships – I started as I meant to go on! At the end of 1984, my Ministox career was coming to a close and I was getting ready to move up to Formula 1. My last car was sold to a young and upcoming driver by the name of Rob Speak.

Ministox racing definitely helps young drivers learn about oval racing; how to give and take knocks, track craft and racing strategies. The kids love it, the only trouble can sometimes come from the over-keen parents!

The grid for the superstars in the Grand National, like all other Shootout races, was decided on the Shootout points totals before the meeting started. That should have left half of the Shootout drivers in front of me, but Paul Hines, Ed Neachell, Mat Newson and Lee Fairhurst did not appear so I only had Mick Sworder and Michael Scriven in front. Mick was electric at the start of the race and was off like a sprinter out of the blocks. I soon passed Michael and was chasing after him. We were both cutting through well and I was really improving my position – by the time there was a caution on the seventh lap I was up to sixth. Mick Rogers was just in front. As we entered the final turn on the rolling lap, he went a little wide. I went for it, nipping up the inside, but taking a tighter line meant that I had to turn a little steeper than usual. John Lund was in front of Mick Rogers and he came from the outside on the racing line, clipping my outside front which sent me into a spin. It was my own clumsiness and hurry to get going and past the lower grader that caused the problem. My spin caused Danny Wainman and Adam Slater to go up the fence, which led the marshals to stop the race again straight away. I could rejoin, but only at the back. With only a dozen cars left in the race, I knew that I'd be able to pick up a few points. I managed seventh place, but again it could and should have been a lot better, just like in the final.

Not a brilliant haul of points again, but the 27 I picked up kept me in the chase and took me to fifth. The cut-off point in the Shootout is after five rounds, when the top six drivers will progress to the second half of the series. It's different to how we've done it before, and it means that, now more than ever, in the first few meetings you can't win the Shootout – but you can certainly lose it. I'm still in there, and I'm not discounting myself.

The Shootout has so many different permutations and tactical possibilities, and that's one of the appealing things about it. At this stage last year, Craig was nowhere. He came through from under the radar to win. That might be the best way to win the Shootout, but maybe this year, somebody will spot the dark horse earlier and deal with him. Somebody might choose to slow the defending champion down on shale, because that's definitely where he's stronger. Maybe they will do it early, rather than leaving it to the last rounds. However, that means somebody needs to take the initiative, and it also leaves them open for payback. And if Craig is eliminated then there are still three or four or more others waiting in the wings. What's the best way to stop Frankie, Tom, Dan, Mat, Mick – or me?

I'd certainly love to win the Shootout. I consider it to be one of the big four titles along with the World, British and European Championships. If I did manage to win it, it would mean that I have a career Grand Slam – and not many drivers can claim that. First though, it was time to concentrate on one of the ones that I'd already won.

Another day, another interview –
the build up to the World Final

17

Could two Harrisons carry the gold roof at the same time?

Bradley won the National Championship for Ministox, their gold roof race, in 2010. He lost the title in 2011, about a week before I won the World Final. Although we had a couple of photos taken before his Mini was repainted with a red roof, we did not actually hold the titles at the same time.

So, the weekend before the World Final, we travelled up to Barford for the National Championship hoping that he might win the title again. The same meeting was also hosting the Formula 2 World Final, meaning it was going to be a busy meeting at a small track. The weather was glorious. Bradley went out for a practice early on. It was the first time he raced on the track which wasn't ideal, but he said he felt like he could manage on it.

Bradley was starting from the fourth row, just like his dad. Frankie Wainman Junior Junior was on pole, just like his dad. Finnikin and Smith were also lining up. Hang on a second, this was looking awfully familiar...

It wasn't to be. Bradley had a good race. He had to battle for position, both defensive and attacking, and finished in fifth. His wasn't the fastest car on track, but his driving was good. Frankie JJ drove a blinder, a performance that was beyond his years. Bradley's consolation was that maybe the next time he drives for a gold roof, it'll be competing against me.

It was getting dark before the Ministox race finished and when he returned to the pits Bradley said, 'Dad, it's really dark out there, I don't want to race again. It feels dangerous.'

It was Bradley's call, I had no problem with it, so when they called for the next Mini race I told them Bradley wasn't racing. Only then did I wander across to the track. Crikey! I didn't blame Bradley one bit for his decision, in fact I completely supported him. I wouldn't have raced out there. Northampton and Skegness can be difficult to see around when it gets dark, but this was far worse. There is no way I would challenge a track as dark as that.

The Minis went out on track, but before they gridded the Ministox chairman took the decision that it was too dark and pulled them off track for the evening. The meeting carried on with the Formula 2 races. It was ridiculous. Drivers went into corners unsighted, a couple would crash and everyone else would follow in because they couldn't see ahead. Thirty cars qualified for the meeting final and only nineteen turned up on track, so plenty of others were of the same thought and took the same decision that I would have.

As a World Final venue, Barford does not measure up. It's nowhere near the standard I would expect. It's effectively on a farm with just a mesh fence separating the spectators from the cows. The floodlights obviously weren't up to scratch, nor were many of the other facilities. Before the Formula 2 World Final, which was run early on the schedule the next day, I heard a chap complaining to his family that he'd queued for half an hour to buy a coffee only to get there and discover that they'd run out of water!

The Formula 2 World Final got going the next day and Mickey Brennan went into the lead after a couple of laps. However, in the first half of the race there were five stoppages. It was farcical. Only when the field had been obliterated and there was a dozen or so cars left did some proper racing go on without hiccups. The trouble was that the track was narrow and there was not much room to manoeuvre, so when the track became half blocked they didn't really have any choice but to chuck the yellows. The parameters of the tarmac did not lend itself to allowing a World Final to flow.

It was a worry that I had about Skegness holding the Formula 1 World Final only a week later. In an ideal world, the green flag would wave in the World Final and it would stay green until the chequered flag. On a bigger track, you can get away with some incidents and cars which might park up off the racing line, but on a track like Barford or Skegness the marshals are forced to halt the race. With 36 Formula 1 cars rumbling around Skegness, I was aware that the World Final might turn into a similar sort of debacle. What were the chances that there would be a full restart? The odds had to be fairly high. What were the chances that the first three rows would get through the first lap unscathed? The odds for that had to be pretty low. I hoped that the race would live up to expectations, but I wasn't sure that it would.

You can't plan for yellow flags or red flags. The World Final that I won had three periods of yellow flags and restarts. It can unhinge you if you're not prepared for them. During the race you have to make decisions depending on what happens. You do all your thinking in the week before the race, but after the first corner who knows will happen and you just have to react to the situation as it confronts you. When the yellows come out, you sit alone in the car and over-think. What shall I do if this happens? What if this happens? Part of the reason that I did so well at Northampton was that I blanked out all those thoughts and focused.

I much prefer to get into a rhythm and momentum. The tyres get some heat in them that way, but when the yellow flags wave, the temperature comes back down. My adrenaline level drops too. Each restart is like the start of a new race and I need two or three laps to get back into it.

All of that was out of my hands. The World Final venue had been decided over a year before, I just had to get on with it and deal with what was within my control.

We had been working on the car since the last tarmac meeting at Birmingham, three weeks before the World Final. Time pressure was off, so there was a lot we wanted to check. Between meetings there is always a general service to check all the nuts and bolts, ensure that everything is tight and nothing is dropping off. But for the World Final I wanted to give everything a thorough going over, especially the bits that had been causing issues over the past few months: clutch, brakes and wheel bearings in particular. I had a concern about the differential after it had gone at the Birmingham meeting before the Shootout round, so we decided to check it over again, taking the half shaft out and removing the front flange of the pinion. We weren't satisfied, it felt notchy as the flange turned, so we obtained another crown wheel and pinion. The half shaft that I had been running was just a shortened Transit half shaft so we decided to get a better option. I spoke with Team Gilbank who supplied me with a new one and when I told them about my concerns with the differential they offered to pop in and have a look the week before the World Final. The diff has to sit perfectly if you want it to have a long life. We really went to town on it with Mark and Brian Gilbank until we were completely happy.

The starter motor had been sent away to get a new solenoid fitted, that was put back in and tested. The engine oil was ready for changing so that was done, and the car needed a good steam clean to get off all the rubbish before it was painted and neatened up. The last job was to weigh it. Despite all the work everything was spot on. The car was loaded up together with the barbeque equipment and a few beers – vital supplies for the weekend!

I'd also spent an evening or two messing with some tyres. I had decided to run a Kumho rally tyre on the front inside wheel, a medium compound which I had been using for a few meetings to get worn in, and a rally tyre that I'd worn in on shale for the rear inside. Now I used a tyre grinder to buff up a nice surface on both, taking off the feather and loose edges that had built up from racing but leaving on a fair tread so they would be good tyres for the entire race.

Everything was as well-prepared as we could reasonably expect. For the first time since the previous World Final, I was confident that there were no issues or niggles that might affect the car.

Loading up on Wednesday meant that I was free to attend the St Leger meeting at Doncaster racecourse on

Thursday. It's often just before the World Final and is a good way to let my hair down and relax. As usual, it was a day with a lot of liquid refreshment and careful studying of the form book – that usually involves picking the best names and numbers!

Horse number 2 came in second in the first race, behind horse number 4 – the reverse order of last year's World Final! Once the betting got in full swing, I did pretty well. Gold Cheongsam (number 22) was a winner, then horse number 2 won the next race and Goldream picked up a place for me a couple of races later. You might be able to deduce my non-scientific method of picking the horses! The winnings were helping to fund the refreshments and I hoped my lucky streak on the horses would continue until the weekend.

The next day, World Final Eve, I felt a little delicate. This time last year, I'd spoken to Mike Finnigan and he'd helped get my head in the right place. This time he sent me a text reminding me to stay focused, but twelve months on from winning I was in a completely different place. Last year I was under a huge amount of pressure. I knew that my time was running out. I was starting on the front row and I was well aware that this might be the best chance I had left to win the World Championship, but the fear of the first lap was preying on my mind. I needed that doubt taking away. Now, I had achieved my ultimate goal to be World Champion. I no longer felt that desperation and need to win – sure, I wanted to win and to retain the title, but it wasn't essential.

We had a quiet evening. Bradley was already in Skegness with my mum and dad for the Friday night meeting. Lindsey, Melissa and I enjoyed a homemade curry and watched a bit of TV, then we had a bit of fun with the trophy. I had some pictures taken with it, including snuggling up to it in bed. It was all good-natured fun and very relaxed.

On the big day I woke up early, although I didn't have any jitters. We intended to leave the yard at 10 o'clock on Saturday morning to get a decent spot in the pits. I got my race suit and fireproofs together in the house while Lindsey packed all the snacks and barbeque meat. I was calm. If anything Lindsey was the tense one, checking round and asking if we had everything. I assured her that we did and we set off to drive the fifteen minutes or so to the yard. As we got there, Lindsey turned to me and said, 'did you get the transponder?' Crap, it was still charging in the kitchen! I was still keen to get going and knew that Lee had a spare, but the bus wasn't to be seen. The rest of the lads, who would normally be sat in it awaiting our arrival, reported that the bus was blocked in. One of the tenants in the yard had parked a big earth mover and a car across the back of it. Lee had already phoned its owner and asked him to move it, and he also sorted out the spare transponder. In the end, we set off about half an hour late. Despite the problems, I was still calm and unruffled.

On arriving at the stadium, I got the trophy and put it by the windscreen as we drove in for everybody to see – at least I hadn't forgotten that after all the fun we had with it the night before! I was keen to get the car unloaded, the aerofoil on and the trophy out for everyone to see. We had a load of promotional postcards to hand out and there was a steady flow of people wanting my signature on them and to have their picture taken with the trophy and with me. There was a bit of extra fuss going on around our section of the pits. Part of the benefit of being the defending champion was this moment – I wanted to give myself to the fans and I was enjoying every minute. Time was flying by.

I wanted to give the car a shakedown in the first practice session just to check that everything was all right. I did a few laps between the two guys from New Zealand so didn't get a chance to compare myself directly with the frontrunners, but the car felt good. To begin with there was a little bit too much rear brake, but I made an adjustment on the bias valve in the cab to take the pressure off and after a couple of laps it felt much better. I reversed back to the bus in the pits and the lads immediately noticed there was an oil leak from the differential. We had a moment to make a decision – should we intervene or leave it? In a normal meeting we might have allowed it to drip, but we decided to drain the oil out and reseal the diff. The pan was taken off and the expensive synthetic oil collected in a clean container, then the pan was scraped clean. I was keen to keep an eye on the others in practice while this was going on so I kept wandering up to look over the wall. Tom Harris looked like he had blistering form and would live up to his billing as one of the pre-race favourites. The plan was to get out again for second practice with two new tyres on the outside wheels, but there just wasn't time. We'd put plenty of sealant on the differential pan when it went back on and it needed a bit of time to set. Eventually, it was time to take the car to scrutineering and then to a secure compound.

Before the meeting started there was a bit of fun entertainment with Formula 1 drivers racing in a family team series in stoxkarts. Mick Sworder and I were asked to be guest commentators and we had a bit of fun with each other. They also asked me, Dad and Bradley to come out on track and give a brief interview to the crowd. I'd never been so busy before a meeting started!

Spectators kept on asking me how I felt; the television crew and the track presentation team were asking the same thing. The bravado I showed before last year's World Final in the pre-meeting interviews was absent. Then, I had announced with no doubt that I was going to win. It was all part of the intense focus that I had, all part of the technique I was using to take the pressure off. This time, I didn't have the same pressure and I didn't want to show the same bullishness. I was quietly confident, but I didn't want to appear arrogant. I got away with it last time, but maybe not twice in a row!

The meeting was about to get started. The first race was the consolation semi-final. That would be interesting. With a closed grid and everybody pushing for the top two places, how the start of this race unfolded would be similar to the start of the World Final. The green flags fell and the cars roared down the home straight, but not much further. There was a big pile-up on the first bend. I couldn't see the start of the World Final being any different. 'How did the inside of row 4 get on?' I joked. With a bit of luck, Mike James started there because once the yellow flags came out he was at the front!

The spectators seemed to be crammed into the stadium and enjoyed a good race which saw Ron Kroonder and Dan Johnson claim the final places on the grid. Lee Fairhurst just missed out again, coming home in third. World Championship luck seemed to have deserted him this year.

I had a quick nosey at the second heat but time was getting on. It was getting to dusk and the World Final was going to be in the dark, as opposed to last year at Northampton when it was still just daylight. I think that the big race looks better under floodlights, it all adds to the spectacle.

Lee and I walked to the secure compound with the trophy and there were still people hanging around the pits wanting a photograph with it and me. Once in the compound, it was a little quieter. Most drivers and mechanics stuck to their own turf, although I had a chat with Ryan Harrison and Danny Wainman. Both said that they just wanted to finish, Ryan had never managed to complete a World Final. Jessy de Bruyn shook my hand and we wished each other luck, although he looked a little anxious about what was coming up. Helen Kaleta, the starter for the race, came across and asked to have her picture taken with me and the trophy. She also looked a little nervous, so I told her, 'do your thing, you're good at it, just try and enjoy it.' She looked at me and said, 'well, exactly the same advice applies to you!' Then in no time we were queued up, ready to be driven out on track by our mechanics.

I got a good reception and was picked up by the crowd. I had stifled the adrenaline until then, but with everybody cheering I let out a big roar as I left the pit gate, flinging my arms in the air and waving the trophy at the crowd. I was pumping myself up. Helen took the trophy off me as we parked next to Danny. Hopefully I'd pick it up again later.

It was time to get strapped into our cars. I asked Lee to check the differential oil situation – he told me it was fine and nothing to worry about. The leak had been sorted. Michael, who is always the tyre man, had told me that I had exactly five inches of stagger, just as I had asked for. The brakes and the clutch problems had all been dealt with. Everything was right with the car. Now it was down to the driver.

'Right, this is the business end of things,' I said to Lee. He gave me a tap on the shoulder and made his way off the track.

Let's dance.

I looked forward. It wasn't far to the front. Frankie was only three cars ahead, I could see Mick Sworder's car on the outside of the front row. Tom Harris and Craig Finnikin were on row 2, Jessy de Bruyn and Gary Castell had qualified as the best foreigners on row 3. That was it. There were a lot more cars behind me than there were in front. But it was a World Final. It didn't matter who was around me, who was in front, who was up my chuff. It's just one race, everybody wants to win it and all the best drivers should be on the track.

The next thing I heard was, 'gentlemen, start your engines.'

This is what it's all about!

18

My body language said it all. I stood with my hands on my hips, utterly pissed off. A glance at my car told the same story. The front bumper was dented, the sideskid was crumpled out of shape, the rear wheel was stuck fast around the metal armour. Twelve months of wearing the gold roof and it had all come to this.

*

I thought that the key to the race would be the first bend. Much as the spectators wanted to see the best drivers battling it out right at the end, realistically one, two or three of the top contenders wouldn't get round the first lap. My aim was to make sure that it wasn't me.

As the rolling laps began, we followed the track girls round to the start-finish line as they carried the trophy. Then we had two rolling laps with fireworks going from the centre green. The smoke was drifting slowly across the track and I hoped that it would clear by the time the race started, the last thing we needed before the first corner was to be heading into a thick fog. I was turning the front wheels heavily and riding with my foot on the brake, trying to get some heat into the tyres. I also had to concentrate on holding the car in low gear. A heavy elastic band holds my gearstick back in top gear so it doesn't jump out if I take a hit from behind, but it means during rolling laps I have to hold it in the lower gear or the tension in the band will pull it into neutral.

We got to the start-finish line again. This was it, the proper rolling lap before the green flag. Slowly down the straight, through the corner, down the back straight; all the time the tension smouldered. We had been told that the race would start at the end of the last turn opposite the pit gate, where a white tyre had been placed on the infield. Still, you never know whether somebody will go early and try and get a leap on everybody else. Frankie slowed the rolling lap right down through the last corner. I was right on the back bumper of Jessy de Bruyn, I could feel Ryan Harrison on my back bumper. I was ready to go, hand on gearstick, but Frankie and Mick weren't ready.

Frankie backed us up even more. He slowed right down. He was making a statement: I'm in charge here. It was uncomfortable. I was getting the force of the cars behind on my back bumper and the back of my car was being lifted slightly.

Then we were released! Frankie and Mick floored their accelerators and everybody else followed suit. I dipped the clutch and pulled the gearstick back into top gear. There wasn't full traction from my back wheels because Ryan was still lifting me, so I slid forward slightly. Jessy lost his back end and I was square on his back bumper, so as he lost it he took me with him and my back end swung towards the fence. I shut off the gas but the pack was still hitting me, which took my back end the other way and swung the front towards the fence. All the time I was being drilled from behind and pushed down the home straight. Back on the accelerator, I tried to straighten up but carried on into the fence at the start of the corner. It whipped my front wheels onto right-hand lock, trapping me against the fence.

I had a moment to realise that I'd blown it. World Final over. I reversed out and managed to pull the steering wheel back to the left as cars were piling in on either side. I drove round the outside of the corner, pushing my way through the cars that were out of sorts and down the back straight, but I was pretty much at the back of the field. I was checking and feeling for everything. The car seemed to be handling ok but I could see flashing orange lights in my mirror, right up my backside. Frankie and Mick were just behind me, I was already almost a lap down.

Down the home straight and I could see that there were cars all over the first corner and the track was as good as blocked. I kept a wide line and coasted to a halt, stationary on the outside of the track. Frankie was leading and couldn't afford to wait. He charged up the inside and into the pile-up. Mick took the same line and I could see loads of other cars following in. On the outside I was relatively safe.

At last, the yellow flags were waved. We'd already been told in the driver briefing that if yellow flags were shown in the first three laps, the steward might decide on a full restart depending on the situation. With the track completely blocked, they decided to show a red flag and start over. We would have ten minutes to see to any damage. Great stuff, I was back in the game!

It was chaos. Cars were trying to disentangle themselves, tractors were pulling others out of the way. I was just concerned about getting down the back straight and close to the pit gate and pushed my way through the car park. Once at the other end of the track, I jumped out and took a look at the car. The outside front wheel was buckled where it hit the fence but I knew from the lap afterwards that it wasn't unduly affecting the handling and I could cope with it. I didn't have a brand new tyre built up on a rim to replace it, so I decided to stick with what I had. The front axle was bent back slightly, again I could manage with it if I had to, but we had ten minutes and might as well make the most of it. The lads charged across from the pit gate and I shouted at them to get the gear to straighten the axle. With the sounds of sledgehammers clattering against metal as everybody else tried to bodge some repairs on their cars, we worked like mad and got the axle back in place. The lads questioned the scuffs on the front tyre, but I assured them that I was happy with keeping it on.

Back in the car, strapped in and harness on, I returned to the grid. One of the officials came across and said that Jessy and Gary would not be rejoining because they had sustained too much damage. I was also told that Mick had no brakes and would be missing and Tom would also not take the restart. Suddenly I was effectively on the second row, only Frankie and Craig remained from the six cars that started in front. Then Tom rejoined on the inside of the second row and Mick took up his place on the outside of the front row.

I saw that as a good thing. They were major opposition, two of the best drivers, but I didn't want to see the field decimated. They might also give me a little cushion if the same happened again. However, with no Dutch drivers on the third row there was a little gap. I was told to maintain a row's length from Tom as is usual procedure in this kind of situation, but that gap could potentially work in my favour. It would give me a yard to get away from the chasing pack on the start. I would need to be on somebody else's back bumper by the end of the straight – I didn't want the same thing to happen as at Buxton, where I left a gap behind Lee Fairhurst and was on the front of the train into the fence – but I thought if I could anticipate the start and immediately close the gap I could be on Tom's back bumper with a car length gap behind me and I could avoid the hit.

Another rolling lap. We were taken round again and cars started to twitch as we approached the end of the back straight. Surely Mick wouldn't let Frankie leave it so long this time?

At a point where I thought that either Frankie or Mick would have gone, we were still wrapped up. Again, I could feel the cars behind hitting my back bumper, pushing me into the gap. It was getting smaller and smaller and smaller. For Christ's sake, just go! Still we crawled round the last centimetres of the corner, almost coming to a halt.

Eventually Frankie did floor it. Engines roared and every car on the grid leapt forward. But since I didn't go of my own accord, rather than having that crucial gap behind me, Ryan was right up my chuff. The drivers on the first two rows had taken a wide line out of the corner but I was still cramped on the inside. I wasn't square on a bumper, and if that remained the case by the end of the straight I'd be hit across Tom's bow, potentially over his sideskid and bonnet, crashing out. I drifted to the right, trying to place my front bumper onto Tom's back bumper to cushion the impact. I had no breathing space.

The pressure from behind was relentless. The push came from several rows back, at least from Mark Gilbank on row 8, through Paul Hines, Louw Wobbes and Ryan Harrison and onto me. The home straight turned into the corner and I was turning the steering wheel left, but the car was going straight forward. I wasn't braking because I knew that if I did that I would just lock up and go forward, but as the fence got closer, I realised I had to try something. I started to apply the brake as Tom went across the front of Craig, just missing him. I wasn't so lucky. I went across the front of Craig's car which embedded in my side while the front of my car hit the fence. Craig's momentum and the bounce of the fence put me back in the right direction, but I was stationary. I could feel hits as others connected with me or Craig, while other cars jolted round the inside of the corner.

Surely they'll throw another red flag? Again, the race hadn't managed to get past the first corner. I put the car in gear and tried to move out of the way to safety, but I could tell that something wasn't right. I could see cars bearing down on me but mine didn't want to get out of the way. I managed to lurch forward about a car length just as I saw Rob Speak hurtling towards me. He turned over and landed on his roof in exactly the place where I'd been about a second before. If he'd landed on me, who knows what the damage would have been.

With a car on its roof, the yellows were quickly waved, but my car was a sick donkey. It felt like steel was rubbing on steel, maybe the bumper was touching the back axle or the differential was damaged. I got out of the car to inspect the damage. Could it be fixed in ten minutes? I might get another chance.

I took off my helmet to hear Richard Kaleta on the stadium tannoy. 'This is a completely different situation to the first start. The track was blocked then, this is just waved yellow flags because a car is on its roof.' My race was shot. Glancing at the damage, the sideskid had dug into the rim of the outside rear wheel. We wouldn't have been able to fix that in ten minutes anyway.

Paul Harrison. Former World Champion.

Quietly contemplating or just pissed off?

19

I went out on track determined to put on a good show in the consolation race, the first one after my disastrous World Final. I knew my car was quick and wanted to prove it on track. This was now my last meeting with a gold roof – at least for this year – and I wanted to do it proud.

The team had quickly dismissed the result in the big race – 'unlucky, you never stood a chance' – and got down to business to get the car ready for the rest of the meeting. The repairs were a little bodged, but I had a point to prove. Rob Cowley was still a fair distance in front when the lap boards came out but I gradually pulled him in. I was going for it. I hit him wide on the last corner – a little harder than I intended, perhaps a sign of the mood I was in – and went on to take the chequered flag.

I was flying in the meeting final too and went on to cross the line in third place. Circumstances were against me, the final was ended early after flames appeared under Danny Wainman's car. I followed Ed Neachell for the last few laps and he was waving his arms out of the cab, signalling that something needed to be done for Danny. I wasn't sure if he could see something that I couldn't, so I held back at a safe distance. I would have beaten Ed to the flag in normal circumstances, there's no doubt about it. He was miffed after the race, claiming that Lee Robinson had jumped the start. He made his feelings clear and the officials were pleading with him not to do anything daft, because in a similar situation earlier in the season he had thrown his trophy to the floor and reversed over it! I'm not sure I helped his mood when I pointed out, 'don't worry Ed, if the race had finished normally you'd still have been second because I would have beaten you!' Ultimately the win was taken off Lee and Ed was promoted to first, which meant that I finished second.

The last time I'd driven a race as well as those two was when I won the World Final. Kind of ironic, I know. But I felt like I had a point to prove.

For the first time since the previous World Final, I was truly focused, in the zone, just as Mike Finnigan would have liked. Of course, I had wanted to win the British Championship, the European Championship, the World Semi-Final and the World Final – but not quite in the same way that I wanted to win that consolation and meeting final immediately after losing the gold roof. Nothing was going to stop me.

If that sounds a little odd, let me try to explain. It all goes back to the fear that I had before the meeting about the World Final being held at Skegness. I was worried that the first couple of corners would be a farce, that too many of the top contenders would not make it past the first lap. I tried my best to avoid being one of them, but it was out of my control. On the first start, I was a passenger, rammed into the fence. On the second start, exactly the same thing happened. I was denied the chance to race.

If I were in sole control of the sport, the Bernie Ecclestone of Formula 1 Stock Cars, I'd make a few changes. One of the biggest is that the World Final would become a weekend event, with races on both Saturday and Sunday at the same venue – always the best one available. It's the premium event in our sport, so it should be held at a premium track with the premium drivers. In the past, we've been lucky to race at great tracks like Odsal. That might have gone now, but we still have the likes of Coventry, although who knows for how long. The FA Cup final is held at Wembley because it's the best stadium. Rugby teams play the Premiership final at Twickenham for the same reason. I think that's what should happen in stock cars too.

To be fair to the promoters at Skegness, they did as good a job as possible of hosting the World Final at their track. They did their best to put on a few extra facilities and entertainment for the spectators and the racing side of things was well organised in the pits. What I was dubious about was the actual dimensions of the track and whether it was capable of hosting such a big race.

I went to Skegness fearful that everything I had put on the line during the season would be undone in the first corner. I qualified on the inside of the fourth row. On any of the more suitable tracks, that should have been a safe place. There is room to get about, to get ready for the first corner, to pick a line. But Skegness is a smaller track and from the flick of the green, there is a short run down to the first corner with 33 cars on top of each other, bumper to bumper, everybody anxious to get going. It was a recipe for disaster.

After the first start, the fastest two Dutch drivers were no longer in the race. Mick Sworder had received enough damage to effectively end his chances of winning and Tom Harris was nursing his car. After the second start, I was out of the race, Craig Finnikin was too. Frankie was damaged. That's not what you want – the top seven qualifiers to be out or struggling before the race has effectively begun.

Once I was out of the race and watching from the centre green, then it turned into a decent stock car race.

Frankie and Tom had both recovered from the two starts and were racing well, despite the issues with their cars. Dan Johnson came through from the back of the grid and dealt with Tom brutally, just as he did last year. The restart after the yellow flags on lap nine was the only opportunity Dan had to stop Tom driving off into the sunset, and he took it and threw his car at Tom. Dan could have won, but Lee Fairhurst – who, remember, hadn't even qualified through the consolation semi-final – was in the right place at the right time and drove a great race to win and become World Champion. He was cautious enough to keep out of trouble and seized the chance when it came his way.

After racing in the Grand National and returning to the pits at the end of the meeting, the first thought on my mind was to remove my gold wing and take it over to Lee. I handed him the wing in the same fashion that Andy Smith had to me twelve months earlier at Northampton. Lifting it above his head, his team and fans gave a cheer of celebration. Lee could now wear a gold roof at Northampton the following day before repainting his own wing. I embraced Lee and Derek and told them to enjoy their moment. Derek told me that the following week, both he and Lee were heading off in separate ways on sunshine holidays. I joked that they would nod off on their sunbeds, then wake with a start, sit bolt upright and think, 'bloody hell, did I just dream that?'

The Fairhursts are a lovely family and great racing team. Lee is an unassuming lad, who after his semi-final disappointment and with the next two World Finals at least being on shale, would not have expected to be winning gold anytime soon. His parents, Derek and Suzanne, are totally-committed to stock cars. Derek is enjoying the twilight years of his racing while giving every opportunity to Lee's racing career. At just 21, one of the youngest drivers to win the title, Lee's achievement is incredible and will go down in stock car racing folklore for the whole load of bizarre circumstances which culminated in his drive to gold.

Some people will look at the race and say that the 2012 World Final was a classic, but I'd have to disagree. Yes, there was a classic story behind the win. Lee only got onto the grid after his father pulled out at the last moment. Derek's car was not 100% for the race and his decision to pull out allowed Lee onto the grid because as the third-placed driver in the consolation semi-final, Lee was the first reserve. I don't blame Derek at all for the decision that he took. If I were put in the same situation later in my career, there is no doubt that I would take the same decision and allow Bradley to race. I'm pretty sure that every stock car racing father would do the same. Added to that, Lee was driving brilliantly in his semi-final at Birmingham and was dreadfully unlucky that somebody dropped oil on the track, and doubly unlucky that his impact with the fence caused the fuel tap to swing closed – a freak occurrence. So to come from being the 33rd and last car on the grid to finish first was a fairytale for the Fairhursts. Is it right that the World Champion can be a driver who came from the back of the grid, who didn't qualify through the semi-finals and didn't even qualify through the consolation semi-final? Well, the rules allow it, and Lee drove a stunning race and is a deserving World Champion.

However, would it have happened elsewhere, at a different track? The fact that Lee was able to win illustrated what I thought was wrong with the World Final being at Skegness. He won because the first two starts eliminated a great deal of the opposition. Jessy de Bruyn, Gary Castell, Craig Finnikin, Rob Speak and I were out, Mick Sworder was as good as out, Frankie Wainman Junior and Tom Harris were struggling. The race winner and second-placed driver came from the consolation semi-final, so did the highest-finishing foreigner, Ron Kroonder in sixth. All started towards the back of the field. Only two drivers who started the race in the top twelve were able to finish in the top twelve. I couldn't escape the logic. So many cars were deposited in the fence in the first two starts that it was much easier, indeed inevitable, that guys would come through the field from the back of the grid.

Was it a great race? It was certainly entertaining with action aplenty, but it was only a stock car race once the field had been cut down by a third and there was room for the cars that remained to race properly, the kind of numbers that the Skegness track can cope with.

The track conditions were great, it was dry and mild, so you would expect the frontrunners to be there towards the end. This wasn't like the Formula 2 World Final at King's Lynn the year before, where Mark Simpson came through from the consolation semi-final to win. On that occasion, a monsoon meant that the track conditions were dire and cars were unable to stay on the racing line. At Skegness, the weather conditions couldn't have been better.

I had done so much work through the year, coming through the qualifying rounds and racing at some tracks that I don't really like going to. In the semi-final I went down to King's Lynn and drove a hard race, taking on Stuart on the last bend to sneak into third. For what? It seemed that qualifying at the front of the grid was a disadvantage.

I would argue that the drivers who have done all the hard work to get to the front of the grid do not deserve their chances of getting round the first corner to be severely reduced in the name of entertainment when they have put in so much effort and sacrificed so much to get there.

With the time and money that goes into racing a Formula 1 stock car, you have to remember that they are not bangers. Yes, it is a contact sport, we all know that. But the rewards are not significant enough to allow our biggest title to go to a track which will result in a destruction derby.

The title means so much to each and every driver that it is inevitable that every driver from the second row to the seventeenth row will be pushing as hard as they can from the drop of the green, potentially resulting in immediate disaster for the drivers at the front.

On a bigger track, I would have been given a chance to get round the first corner. I might not have managed it. I might have hit the fence again, but the odds would have been more in my favour. At Skegness I was ploughed into the fence, not once, but twice. They could have tried another ten restarts and on each of them I'd have been flying by the seat of my pants. The frustrating thing was that I couldn't do anything about it. I was relentlessly pushed from behind into the fence, and I was always going to be, because of the parameters of the track. I felt cheated of the opportunity to defend my title. If I was going to lose it, fair enough. But at least give me a chance.

So, when it came to the consolation and meeting final on World Final night, I felt like I had a point to prove and was determined to drive my socks off.

*

I hope that I don't sound bitter, like a sore loser, because I'm not! I'm giving my heartfelt opinions while writing this less than a week after the World Final meeting. Maybe the pain will go away with time, maybe I'll shrug my shoulders (once they've stopped aching from hitting the fence) and look on the bright side. I'm now a former World Champion, and I'll be happy to call myself a former World Champion for the rest of my life – although I hope that I can be the actual World Champion again some day. But even if that doesn't happen, former World

Champion sounds good. I achieved my life's ambition in fantastic circumstances, and that can never be taken away from me.

But I feel that I have unfinished business. Now I'll have to start again. Work my way through the qualifying rounds, onto a grid at a semi-final, come through that, then the hard work really begins at another World Final. I'm now in my forties and time is ticking by.

Will I race next year? Yes.

Do I know when I'm going to retire? No.

However, I don't think I'll be racing in my fifties. The time to call it a day will be when I feel that I'm no longer capable of mixing it at the top. I'm disappointed in my results this year, although I feel that's due to car reliability more than my own performance. Hopefully, I can have a good run in the Shootout and that will give me a spring-board into next season.

I'm disappointed in the way that I lost my title at Skegness. I want to get back on a World Final grid and give it another crack, to make up for not having a chance to defend my title properly. Maybe that will give me the drive and focus I need, the kind of desire that I showed at Northampton in 2011 and at the consolation and meeting final in Skegness. I need to keep that with me.

Maybe my time will come again.

My Time Is Done

Well the world was won,
I was champion at last;
My dream achieved,
my ambitions surpassed;
My black and white checks,
my British Championship denotation;
Would have to be painted over,
'cos gold was my promotion;
So both my cars wore gold paint,
with stripes on the roof,
I was British and World Champion,

up there was the proof;
Having won my titles,
I was determined to race well;
But that's easier said than done,
as others before me could tell;
I felt no more pressure,
only pride as the Shootout began;
'Cos I was a double champion now,
and my gold roof said I was the man;
In a perfect world I would win silver,
National Points Champion to boot;
But I had to be both lucky and good,
with nine other drivers in the shoot;
Alas despite my best efforts,
the silver I didn't win;
Though it went to the wire,
and was won in style by Craig Finn;
But my season didn't finish too bad,
at the awards night with a beer;
And the icing on the cake,
was being voted driver of the year;
Another opportunity came knocking,
invited to New Zealand to race;
At Rotorua and Palmerston,
getting bashed all over the place;
In no time it was March,
when our season kicks off in the cold;
I waited 'til April when warmer,

maybe a sign I'm getting old!
My enthusiasm was lacking,
my motivation not quite the same;
I questioned if winning the World title,
and achieving my dream was to blame;
I just didn't seem to have any luck,
results were slow coming my way;
Getting damage I wasn't used to,
and thoughts I'd be happier staying away;
I looked towards the main events,
European, British and World title;
Yet I failed miserably at the Euro,
when decent brakes were vital;
I acquired a new shale car from Dave Riley,
built by Tom Harris Motorsport;
'Cos mine was getting dated,
I'd be faster with a new one I thought;
I debuted it at the British Champs,
and couldn't stop it from overheating;
Pulling off in the final just my luck,
as Craig Finn gave us all another beating;
The semis were next,
King's Lynn outside row 2 my berth;
A steady race no drama to report,
a third place finish was all I was worth;
At the Birmingham semi,
Wainman, Tom, and Sworder the master;
Newson and Fairhurst both front runners,

not qualifying was for them a disaster;
The scene was set, the World grid decided,
all roads leading to Skeg Vegas;
Who would victor on the tight little track,
would the Dutch at last upstage us?
The consolation semi the first race out,
to decide who joins the grid at the rear;
Ron Kroonder wins, Johnson second,
Fairhurst missing out for another year;
But by a twist of fate,
Lee gets a chance when father Derek's car turns poorly;
And so as first reserve he joins the parade,
to just make up the numbers surely?
Strapped in our cars, ready to go,
we hear gentlemen start your engines;
But unlike every year I've experienced,
today there are no tensions;
A slow rolling lap, we're all bunched up,
all drivers impatient and tense;
The green flag drops and off we roar,
and I'm one of the first in the fence;
But the track gets blocked, red flags are shown,
the race will be restarted;
Though the next start is no better for me,
as I'm one of the first departed;
The first few laps are a frenzy,
with chaos and smashes a plenty;
In no time at all the grid is dispersed,

from over thirty to less than twenty;
Through all the chaos,
the last two cars battle it out at the front;
As Fairhurst bashes Johnson wide,
in a race-deciding shunt;
217 Lee Fairhurst wins,
from the last car on the grid it's amazing;
At 21 one of the youngest winners,
an achievement well worth praising;
Not quite the race that I'd hoped for myself,
I wanted to retain my title;
But as everyone knows in order to do that,
getting round the first corner is vital;
As the dust now settles on my twelve months as champ,
I can look back with affection;
Alas my results were poor and my luck was bad,
I think that's an honest reflection;
Now a former World Champion who wore the gold,
my reign has just expired;
Though my name is on the trophy at last,
along with the greats I've always admired.

The Harrison Racing Team – from left to right:
Malcolm, Guy, Michael, Bradley, Me, Dad, Lee, Brian,
Joe (or Brian!), Mark (Sid).
Bit gutted that Ray couldn't make the photo call!

Acknowledgements

2011 was the year that I eventually climbed my Mount Everest, found my elusive pot of gold at the end of the rainbow, located my holy grail. I was beginning to think that winning the BriSCA Formula 1 stock car Championship of the World was my impossible dream, something that only other people would achieve.

I had seen others do it. Some were legends of a bygone era, people I had looked up to and admired. Then, as time went on, it was people who had entered the sport just before me. Then just after me. Then long after me! They were friends, people I had grown up with, made mud pies with in the pits as our dads fought their own battles on our fields of dreams.

I always knew I was good enough to win, but whether the enormity of what it meant to me actually worked against me, I can't honestly say. It didn't feel like it at the time, but looking back, I don't think I ever went out on track in a World Final with the correct attitude: with will and desire, the determination that I was going to win, to be the best driver in the best car. Not until 2011.

A twenty-minute phone call with Mike Finnigan the night before the World Final, previously mentioned in this book, was the only difference in my race preparation from victory in 2011 and the previous 22 disappointments.

Maybe he didn't tell me anything different to what I had heard many times from my mum and dad, my wife and sister, my team and my mates, even my children, but surely they were all just saying it because that's what you say to someone that you believe in, knowing what they are capable of and what they can achieve.

Mike Finnigan was different. He didn't know me, had never met me, yet he was able to do something that changed the way I thought that day. He made me believe in myself, somehow he flicked a switch that made me see things differently. I went to Northampton in 2011 with a new found confidence, a different attitude, one that made me the World Champion.

Thank you Mike.

That phone call would never have taken place had it not been for my very good friend Iain Holden who arranged it. I have known Iain since adolescence, since before he and Cecil were winning the World Final as part of the team of the late Ray Tyldesley in 1989. Iain knew what it meant to me, and also knew that I needed a kick up the arse that day in London, the day before the World Final.

Cheers, pal.

Specials mentions must also go two other good stock car mates, Andrew Smith and Peter Falding, who between them have won nine World Finals. I guess I had to win eventually so they could no longer take the piss! Thanks also to Andrew for blowing up my backside and saying something nice for the back cover.

Thanks guys.

I have raced stock cars for 27 years now and I know the score. There are three main ingredients which you need to win the World Final, each in varying doses depending on how things go on that particular day: good driver, good car and good luck. One of these ingredients may be needed in a larger dose than another, but rest assured, to some degree you always need all three.

To get a good car and to be at a lot of the meetings throughout the season and you need the back up of a good team – lads who are prepared to give up their evenings during the week and get grief from their wives or girlfriends when they can't take them to a party on a Saturday night because they will be laid in a puddle of mud under the back of a car with rain running down their neck. I give you medals as thanks for your commitment. They take the form of bashed fingers and thumbs, cuts, bruises and bags under your eyes thanks to the late nights!

Seriously fellas, without you, our successes of 2011 and the fun we had along the way would not have been possible. Thank you, you have all been great.

Ray has given over forty years valued service to Team Harrison. Michael, Ray's son, is Mr Keen on the team, nearly thirty years after first being carried on the coach in his carry cot. Lee has been on the team over thirty years from childhood and became Melissa's godfather. Mark (or Sid) has nearly thirty years of service since a boy and is the son of the late Steve Froggatt, tragically killed in a racing incident at Bradford.

Brian has tirelessly steered our coaches for thirty years while the rest of us are either talking the talk or sleeping off our pints and fish and chip supper (or pork and chips after Cov!) Malcolm is our reserve coach driver and chief tyre fitter.

Raceday help also comes from Glen, Guy, and Joe, who is actually called Brian but changed his name to Joe for us because he didn't want to confuse us because we already had a Brian on the crew. We didn't learn this until much later when one of his mates referred to him as Brian and we didn't have a clue who he was on about, and even

Joe/Brian doesn't know where he came up with the name Joe from!

Callum is the young blood in the team who has come on board to learn the ropes along with my son, Bradley. And let's not forget Jonathan, the Chief-Deck-Chair-Putter-Outer.

Also a mention for Guy's girlfriend Melissa, who always brightens the mood with her smile, and her sidekick, Big Gay Keith. Speaking of whom, no matter how many times you ask, I will not let you hug me better after a disappointing result, neither will I allow you to polish my helmet. If I want it cleaning, I'll clean it myself, thanks!

There are also many team members from the past who helped me on my journey to become World Champion. There's Rocky, named such as he fought off some piss-heads who showed us a distinct lack of courtesy when we were trying to buy our regular post-meeting fish supper – and he had a full arm in plaster at the time. Rocky's late father, Alf, was my dad's drinking companion and Peter Falding-hater. He hated him even more if Peter caused me a post-Friday night hangover!

There has also been Dicky, Dobbo and Ed; and Warren who raced with me in the early nineties, and his team (well, drinking team) including Jonathan and my good friend, Anthony, who I learned to fly jumbo jets with! A few years later Chris Walker raced with me, but he and his wife Ailsa couldn't wait to get away from the madness by emigrating, first to Australia and then Canada!

Andy Maynard from Hi-Spec has not only looked after my engines during my year of success, but has also helped look after Bradley's Minis. Geoff, our welder, pops in if there's anything needs sticking back on – but I usually drive very carefully, so as not to trouble him too much! We're also occasionally helped by my old mate Dean, my very first mechanic then drinking partner, who still can't help getting stuck in if he is at a meeting, even if he is wearing Armani jeans, a Hugo Boss shirt and a pair of Ray-Bans!

I should also thank my employees. Apologies to them if I am a grumpy git after a bad weekend!

Anyone else I should have thanked but haven't mentioned by name, I thank you also and appreciate your efforts.

I was aware of Scott Reeves through his book *Gold Top: The John Lund Story*, so when he first approached me soon after winning the World Final at Northampton, asking if I would be interested in writing a book for Chequered Flag Publishing, I was a little inquisitive. However, I had only recently agreed with Keith Barber that he should write my dad's story in what would become *The Harrison Dynasty*. I was keen to work with Keith because I believe that a lot of people have a story worth telling. While many go untold, I thought that Dad's was definitely worth pursuing. But I also decided that my part in Keith's book would only be as a passing chapter and that writing my own book and putting to print in my own words the experience of my time as World Champion was a venture that I'd get a lot of pleasure out of.

So, in helping me put together and editing my memoirs – which are truly my own words and the product of my own, very slow typing – thanks Scott for your time, your efforts and your patience.

Thanks also to the rest of the team at Chequered Flag Publishing: Chris Parry, Gary Reeves and Roisin Reeves, and also to Mike Greenwood for providing photographs for this book.

It's a varied bunch of people you meet at stock car meetings. The bloke and his wife who he courted at meetings in the fifties and sixties. The people who have cadged a lift with their mate and can barely afford the entrance fee. The affluent businessmen who wouldn't be out of place sat with the panel in *Dragons Den*. The young ladies I remember as toddlers, who I have seen grow up and been introduced to their boyfriends. The young lads who I have seen join other teams, just happy to be a part of our world. My mates with whom I've grown up, started racing in Ministox and moved on to stock cars. Their parents, brothers and sisters, wives and girlfriends. The driver who goes on to promote. The fan who becomes a flag man, starter, steward, tractor driver, photographer, magazine editor, race part supplier. The list goes on and on, but all are ultimately just fans.

Your support, your friendship, your sponsorship, your cheers and boos make our sport what it is; sharing with us the highs and the lows, and helping to make our sport the most exciting and uniquely friendly motorsport imaginable.

Thank you, each and every one of you.

One last thing. Putting into words how much my family means to me. Have you ever tried that?

My mum and dad: everyone at stock cars loves my mum and dad because they are wonderful people. I love you with all my heart and am proud to be your son.

My sister Vicky, my part-time business partner and my friend. They say you can't choose your family, well, I would have chosen all three of you every day of the week.

My gorgeous wife Lindsey. My best friend and my soulmate. I like you a lot!

My beautiful children, Bradley and Melissa. I am proud to be your dad and you both make my heart sing. May you live to be as happy as I am.

I love you all very much, to the moon and back again. Between you, you have helped to make me who I am. Your love and support, patience and understanding have allowed me to live as I do, and to ultimately achieve my dream. I am glad that you were all there to share it with me.

Thanks for everything.

I'd like to thank the following companies for their help and financial assistance during my reign as World and British Champion:

Broadway Van Sales
CW Autos
Firow Propshafts
Hi-Spec Race Engines
Racequip
Richard Baldwin Motorhomes
Searles Leisure Resorts Hunstanton
Skegness Stadium
SPX Service Solutions
Teng Tools
Tom Harris Motorsport
www.stockcarmakelaar.nl

And my own companies:

Meadowhall Transport Ltd
Merlin Trucks Ltd

Results

	Heat	Cons	Final	GN	Other
Sat 10 Sept Northampton World Championship	**1st (World Final)**				
Sun 11 Sept Northampton	DNF				
Sun 18 Sept King's Lynn	**1st**, 4th		2nd	3rd	
Sat 1 Oct Coventry	2nd		DNF	DNF	
Sun 9 Oct Sheffield	DNF, 3rd		10th	DNF	
Sun 16 Oct Belle Vue	8th, 5th		2nd	4th	

Sat 22 Oct Birmingham	DNF	6th	DNF	DNF	
Sun 23 Oct Northampton	3rd		DNF	5th	
Sat 29 Oct King's Lynn	6th, 4th		3rd	9th	
Sat 5 Nov Coventry	DNF	3rd	DNF	5th (GN Champ)	8th (World of Shale)
Sun 13 Nov Belle Vue	5th, 12th		4th	4th	
Sat 14 Jan Rotorua, NZ World 240 Championship	8th, 7th, 9th				
Sat 21 Jan Palmerston North, NZ 248 Global Challenge	DNF, 9th, 9th				
Fri 6 Apr Skegness	7th, DNF		5th	4th	
Sat 7 Apr Coventry	5th		5th	DNF	
Sat 21 Apr Birmingham	4th		6th	4th	
Sun 22 Apr Hednesford	6th, DNF		3rd	6th	
Sat 28 Apr King's Lynn	3rd		9th	5th	
Sun 29 Apr Belle Vue	DNF, 6th		5th		

Sat 5 May Coventry	4th		9th	4th	
Mon 7 May Sheffield	5th, 2nd		4th	7th	
Sat 12 May Skegness	3rd		DNF		
Sun 13 May Skegness UK Open	4th, 4th		5th		
Sat 26 May King's Lynn	10th		6th	8th	
Sun 27 May King's Lynn	8th		DNF	DNF	
Sat 2 June Coventry	5th		5th	**1st**	
Sun 17 June Buxton	7th, 6th		DNF	6th	
Sat 30 June Skegness	DNF, 7th		DNF	4th	
Sun 1 July Skegness	8th, 10th		9th		
Sat 7 July Coventry British Championship	5th, DNF		DNF (British Champ)		
Sat 14 July Northampton	DNF	5th	6th		
Sun 15 July Northampton European Championship	9th		DNF		DNF (Euro Champ)
Sat 21 July King's Lynn World Semi	3rd (World Semi)		DNF	2nd	

Sat 28 July Birmingham	DNF			11th	
Sat 4 Aug Coventry	12th	2nd	DNF	4th	
Sat 25 Aug Birmingham	DNF, DNF		4th	6th	
Sat 1 Sept Coventry	3rd		7th	7th	
Sat 15 Sept Skegness World Championship	DNF (World Final)	**1st**	2nd	7th	

Buy copies of the images in this book from

Mike Greenwood's Photostox
www.photostox.com

www.chequeredflagpublishing.co.uk